# THE

# UNLEGENDARY

# ARTIST

## THE ART AND RANDOM FUN OF AN UNKNOWN

COMPOSED + ILLUSTRATED

BY

SCOTT DAVIS

WWW.DAVISSTUDIO1.COM

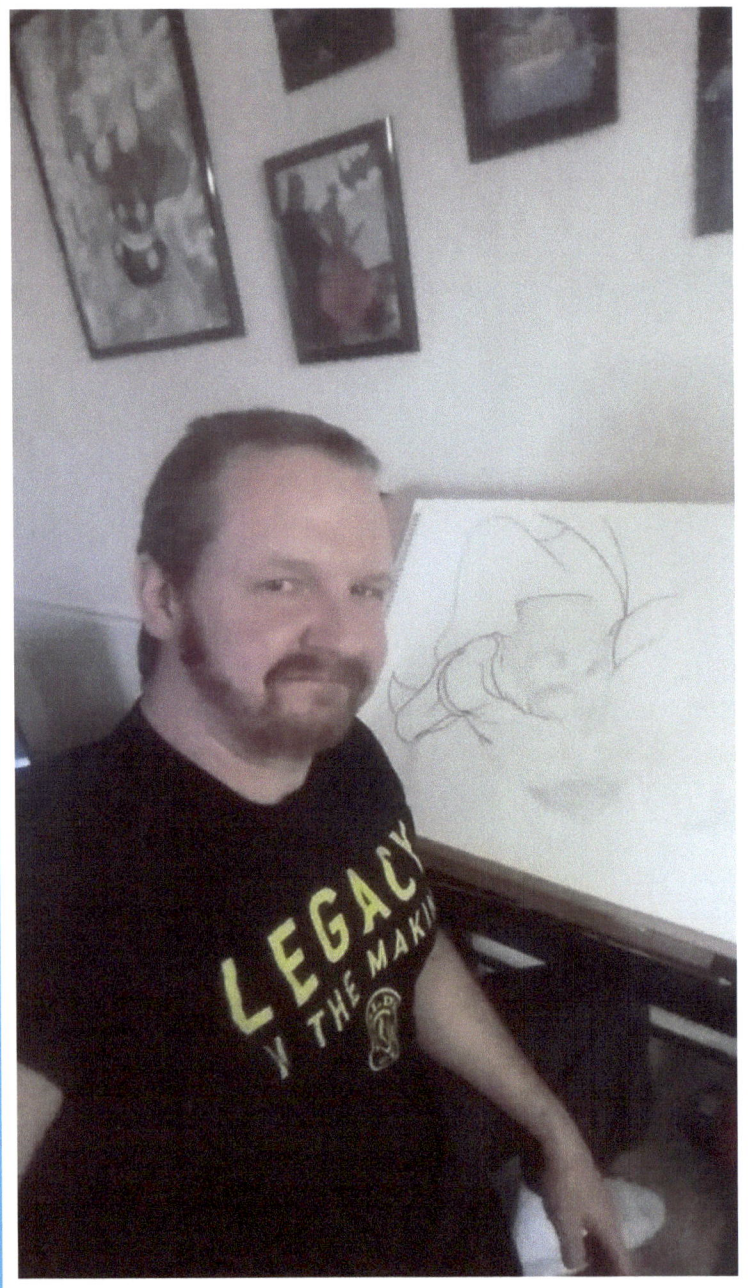

Welcome to my first compilation of work from my drawing board, and sketchpad to you. The pieces you are about to view, some unfinished but noteworthy, are, as some would say, a large part of me. There is nothing I do that doesn't have a piece of my love for the genre that particular piece portrays. I hope you enjoy my work, and that it is a welcome addition to your library, and that if you yourself are an artist, that you will never quit no matter what.

-S. Davis 2016

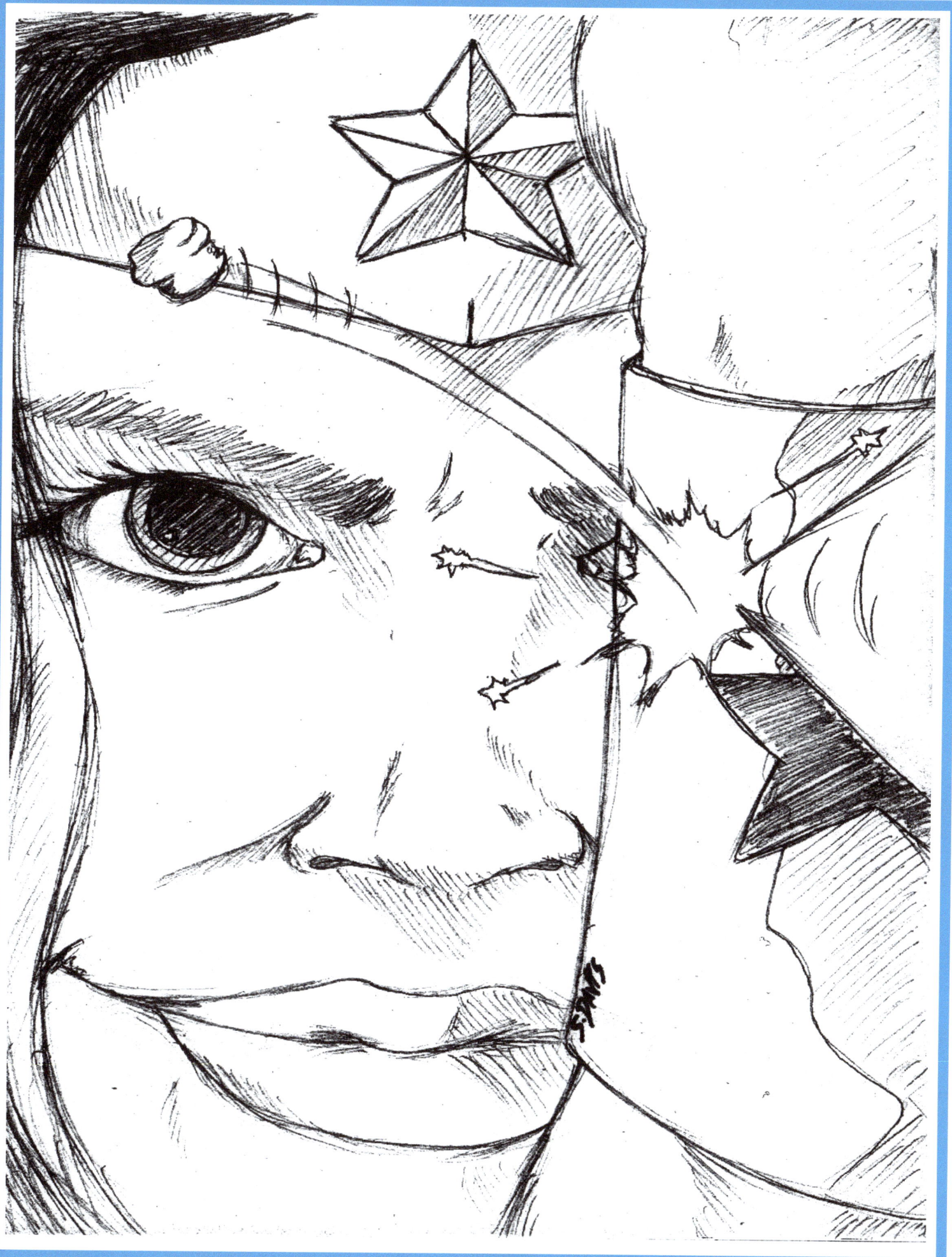

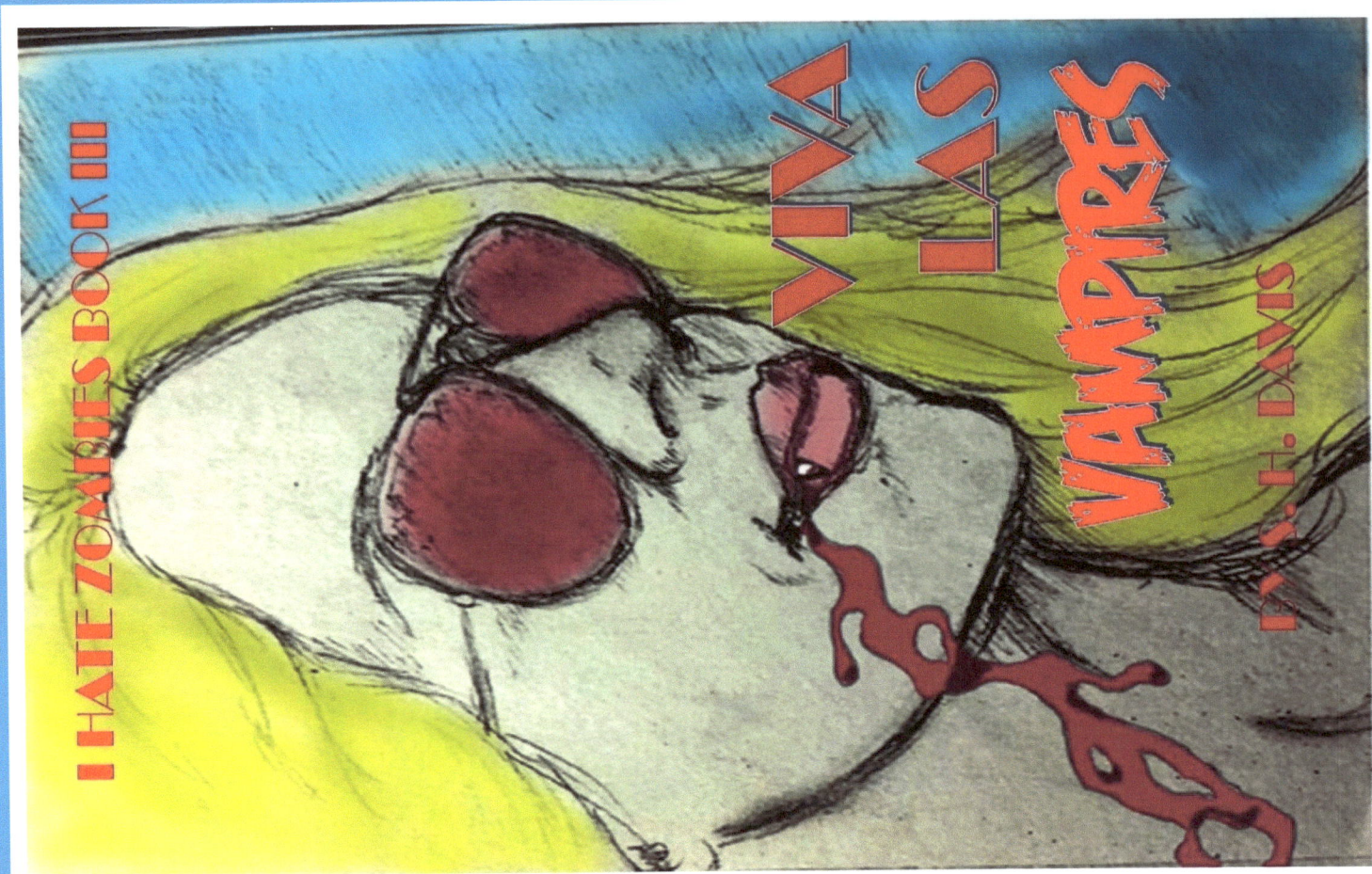

I HATE ZOMBIES BOOK III

VIVA LAS VAMPIRES

VIVA LAS VAMPIRES

BY S. H. DAVIS

VIVA LAS VAMPIRES is an adventure of the most predatory nature. The Nosferatu (vampires), surrounded by both their zombie and beastly minions, have claimed Sin City as their new territory, and the human race has fallen back to their underground bunkers to regroup trying to solve Lord Jolenak's end game.

In the middle of it all, on what he hoped would be a simple quest to find his kid-napped lady friend Darcy, is the one and only Sergeant Akins. Armed to the teeth, as stressed out as ever and hunted by things nightmares would flee from, our would be hero is about to go all in for a game where the odds are definitely NOT in his favor.

So lock and load, sharpen those wooden stakes and say a prayer, because this time it goes for the jugular!

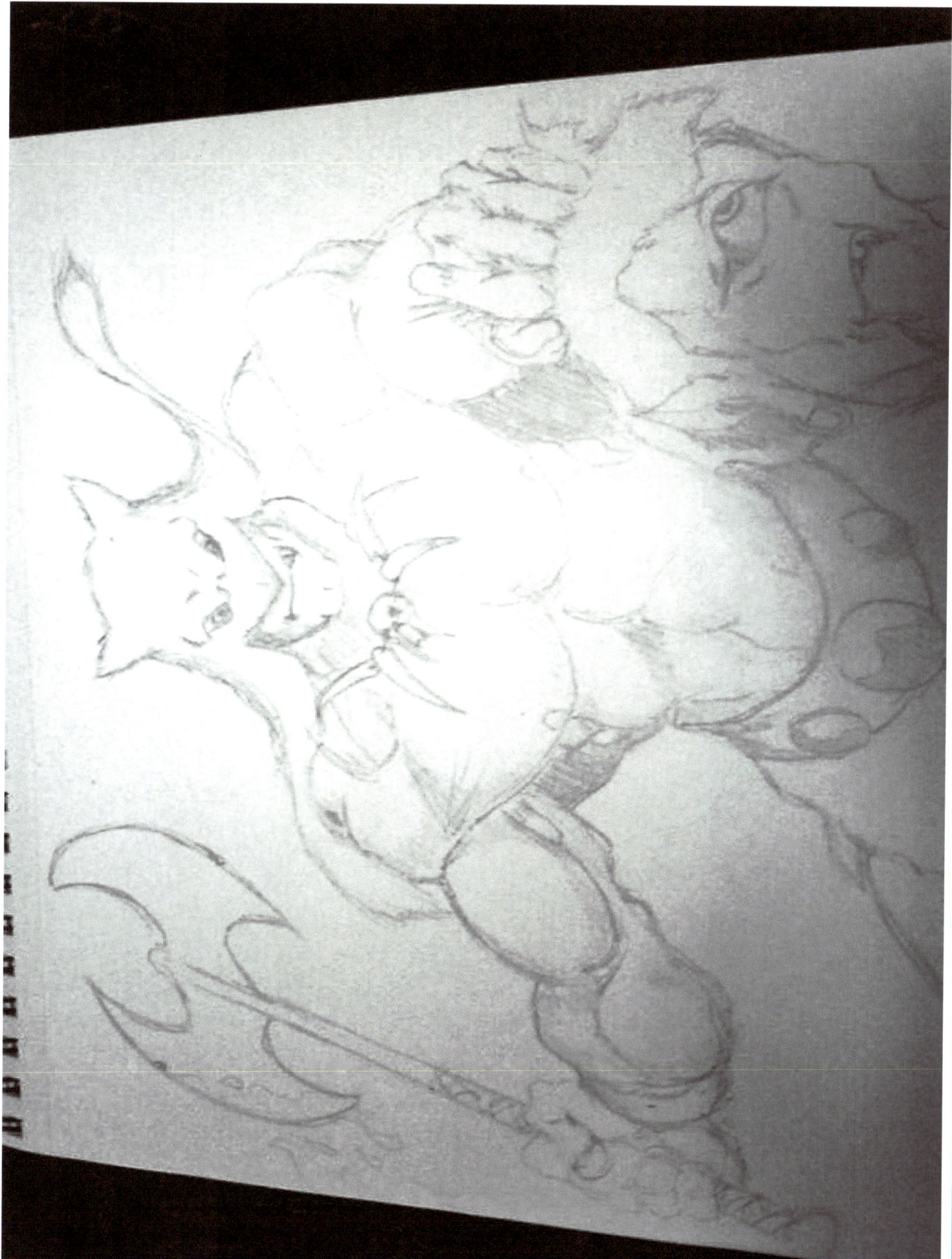

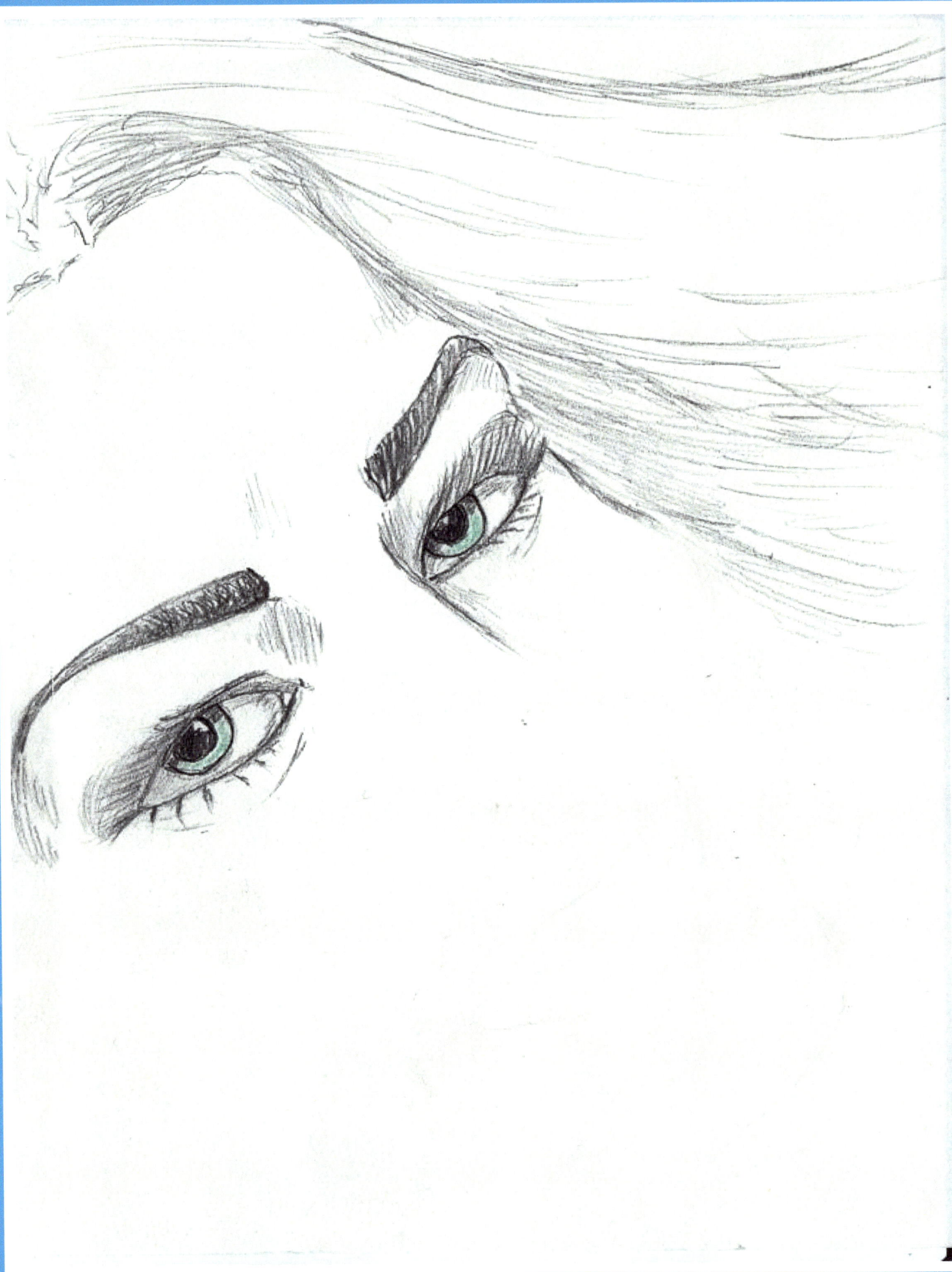

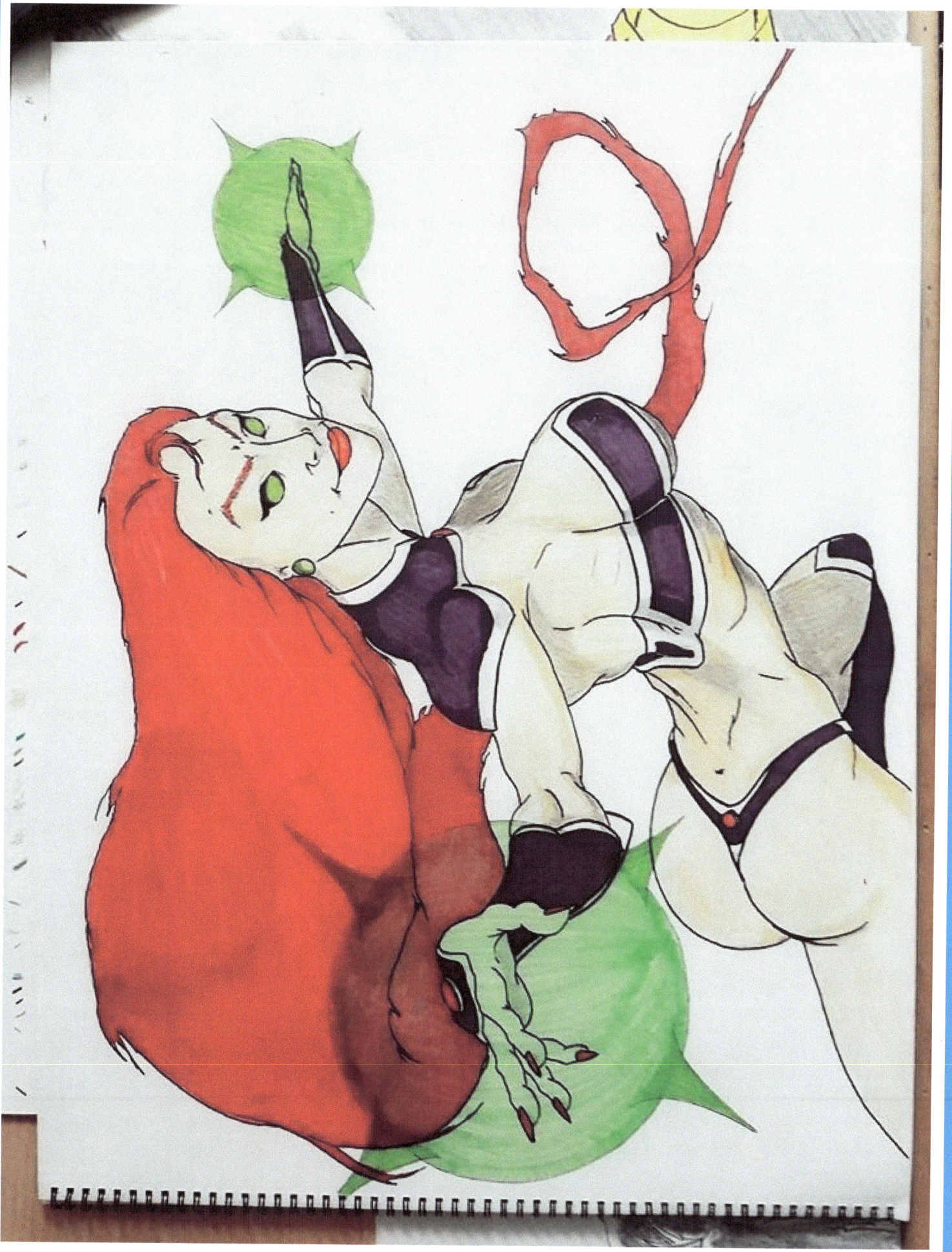

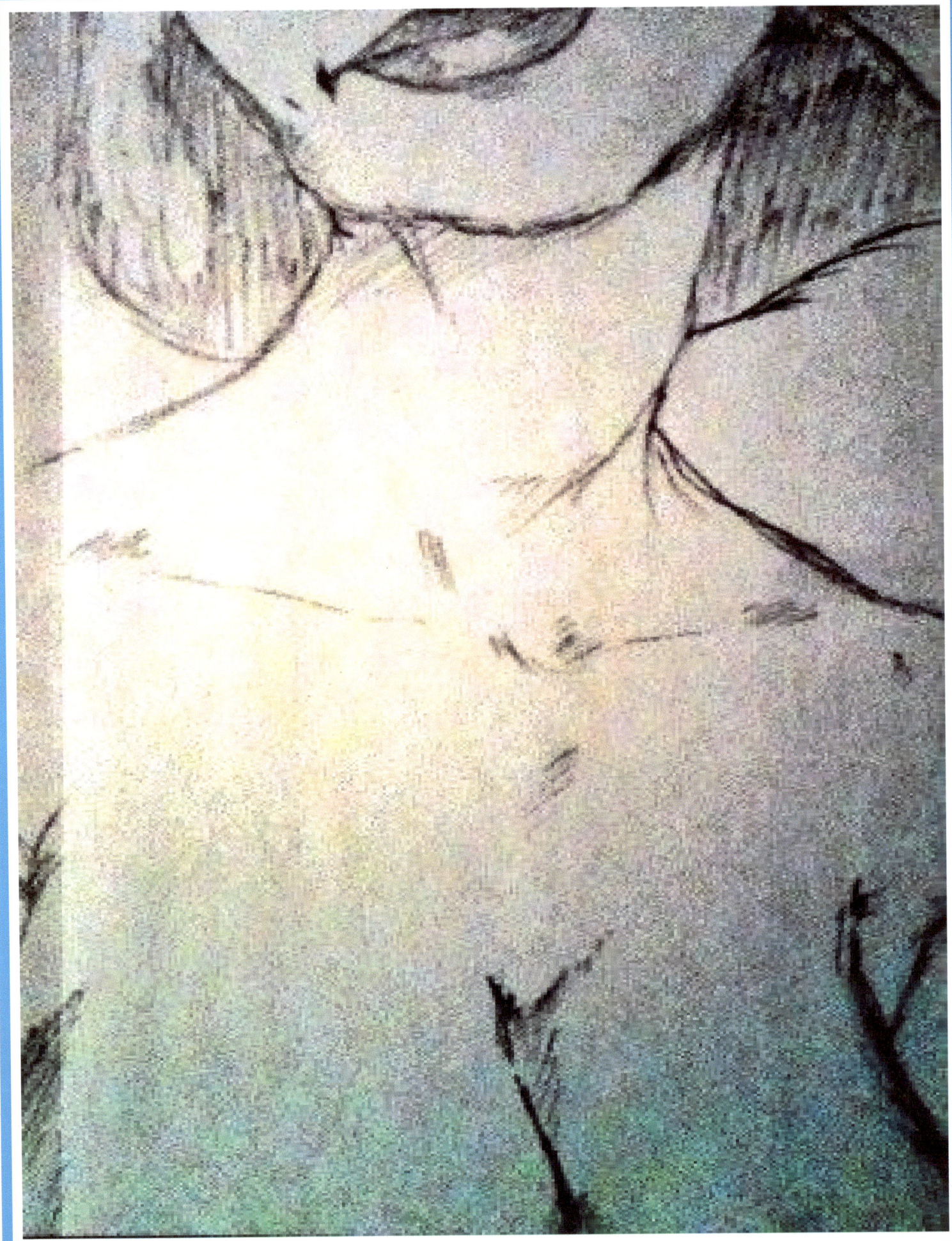

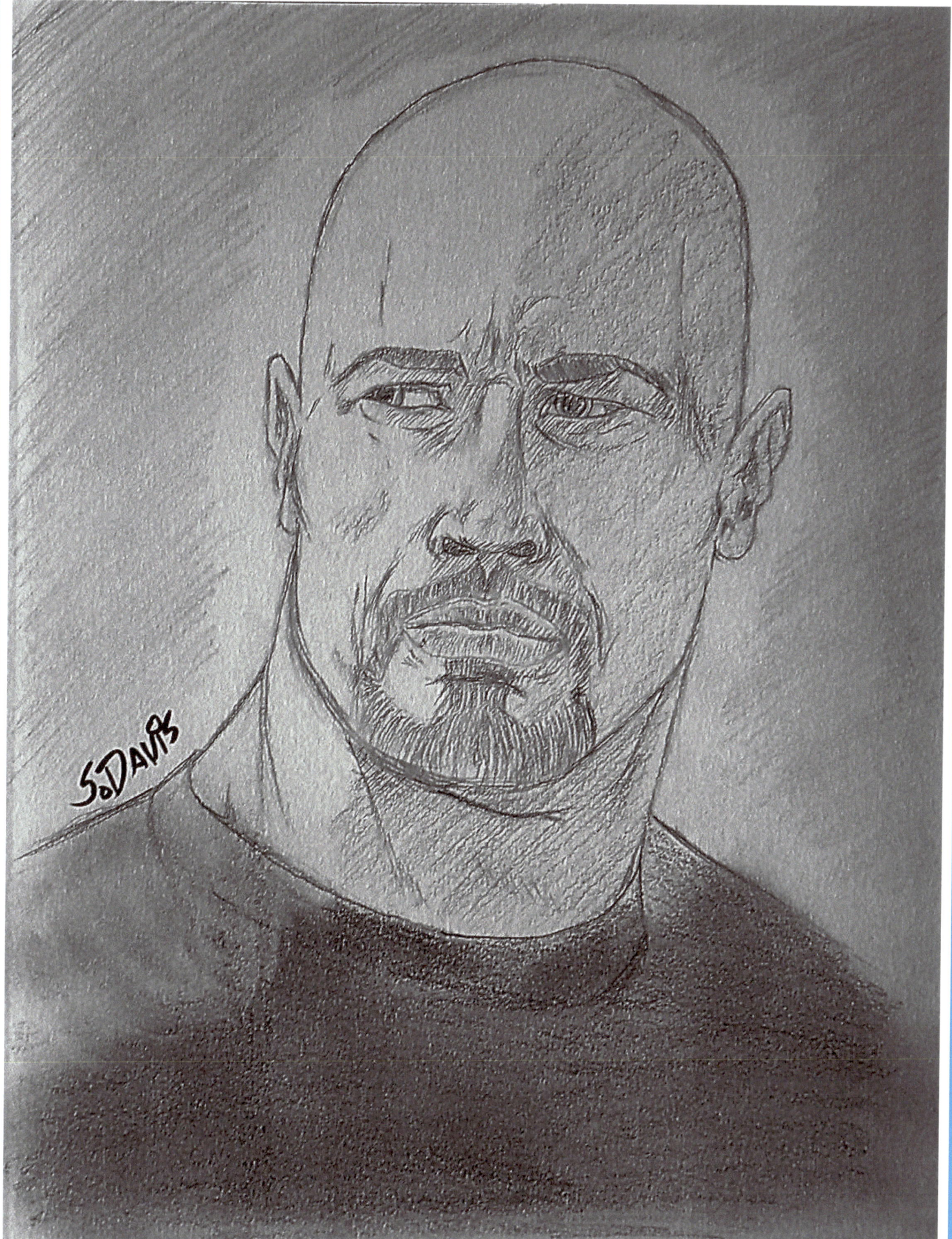

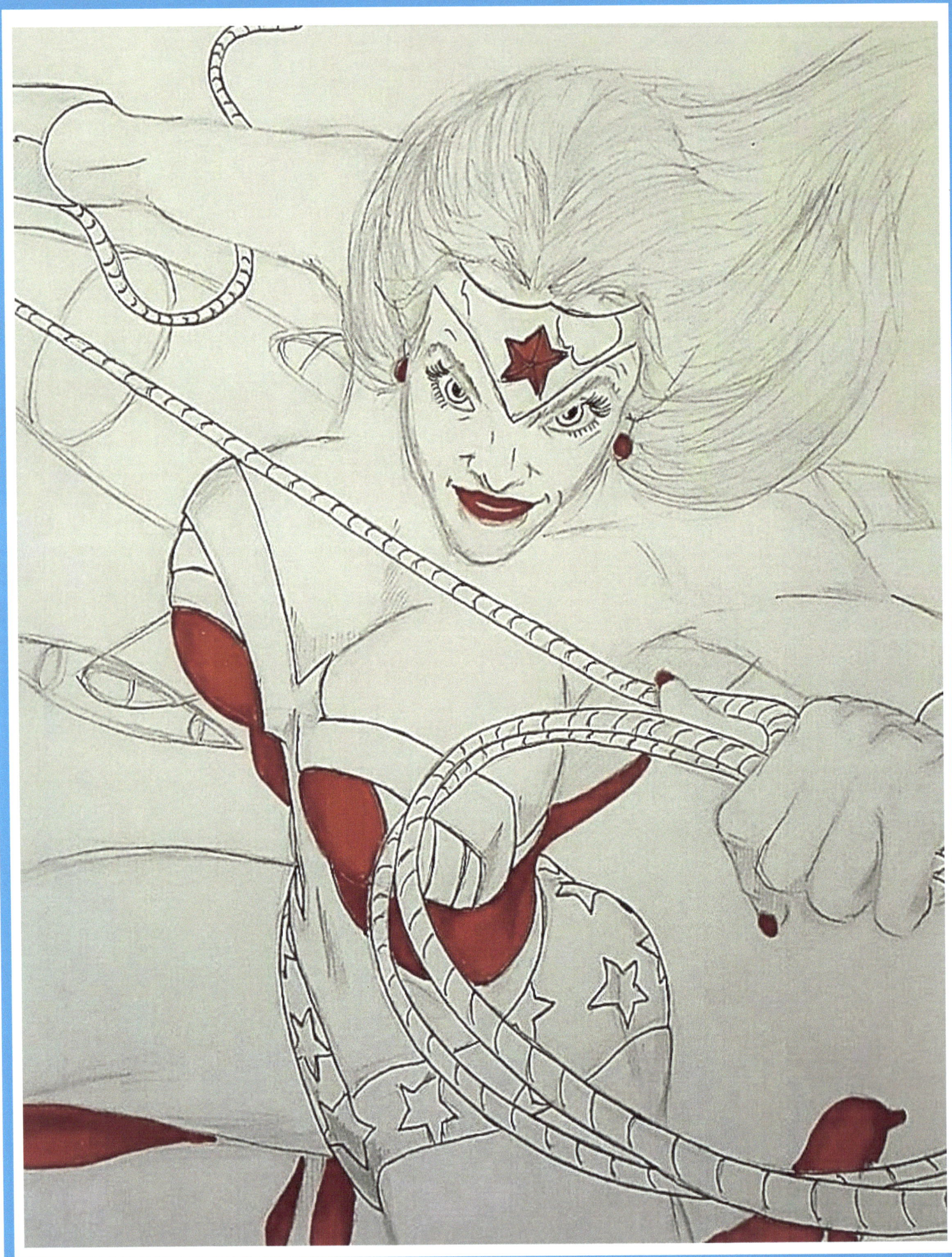

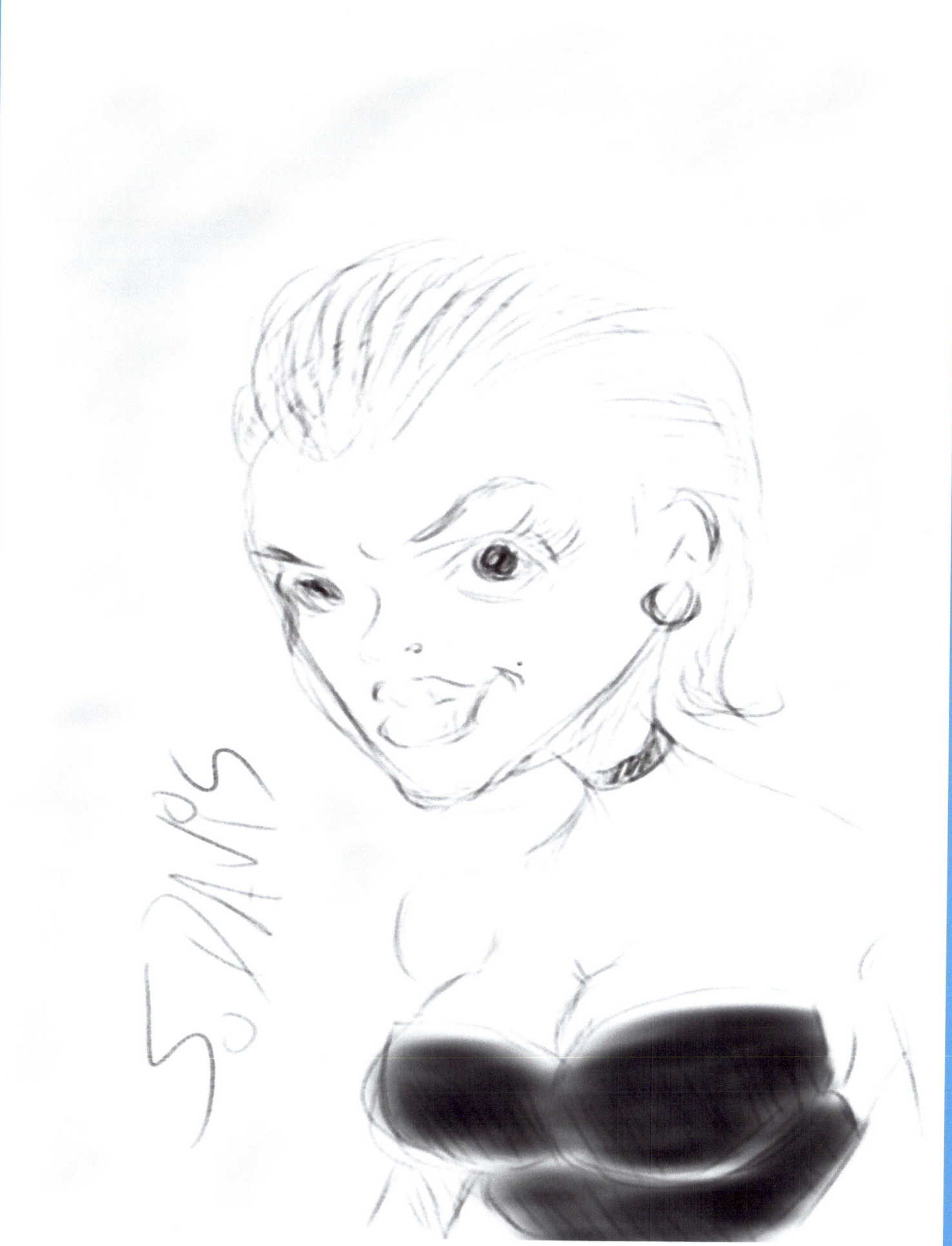

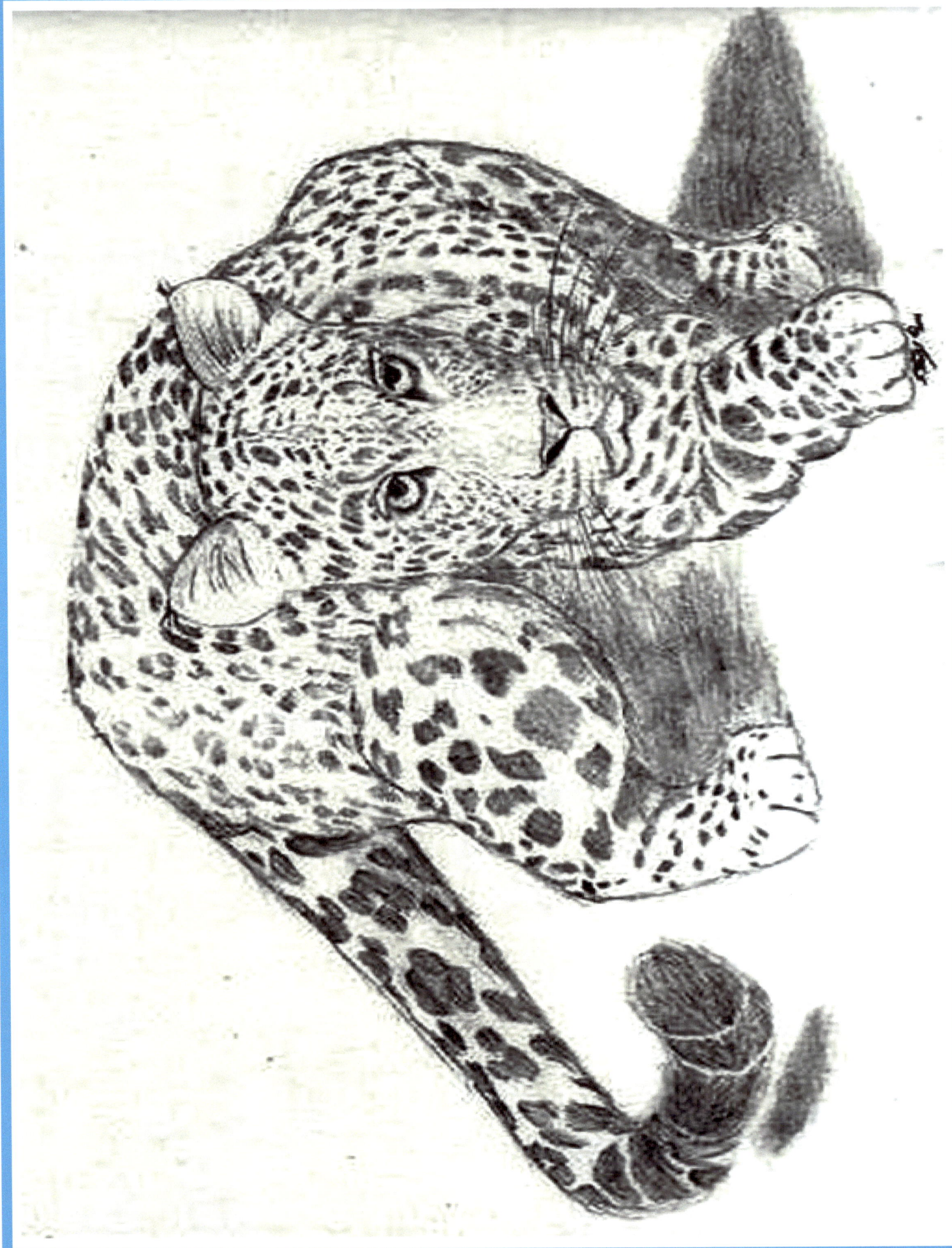

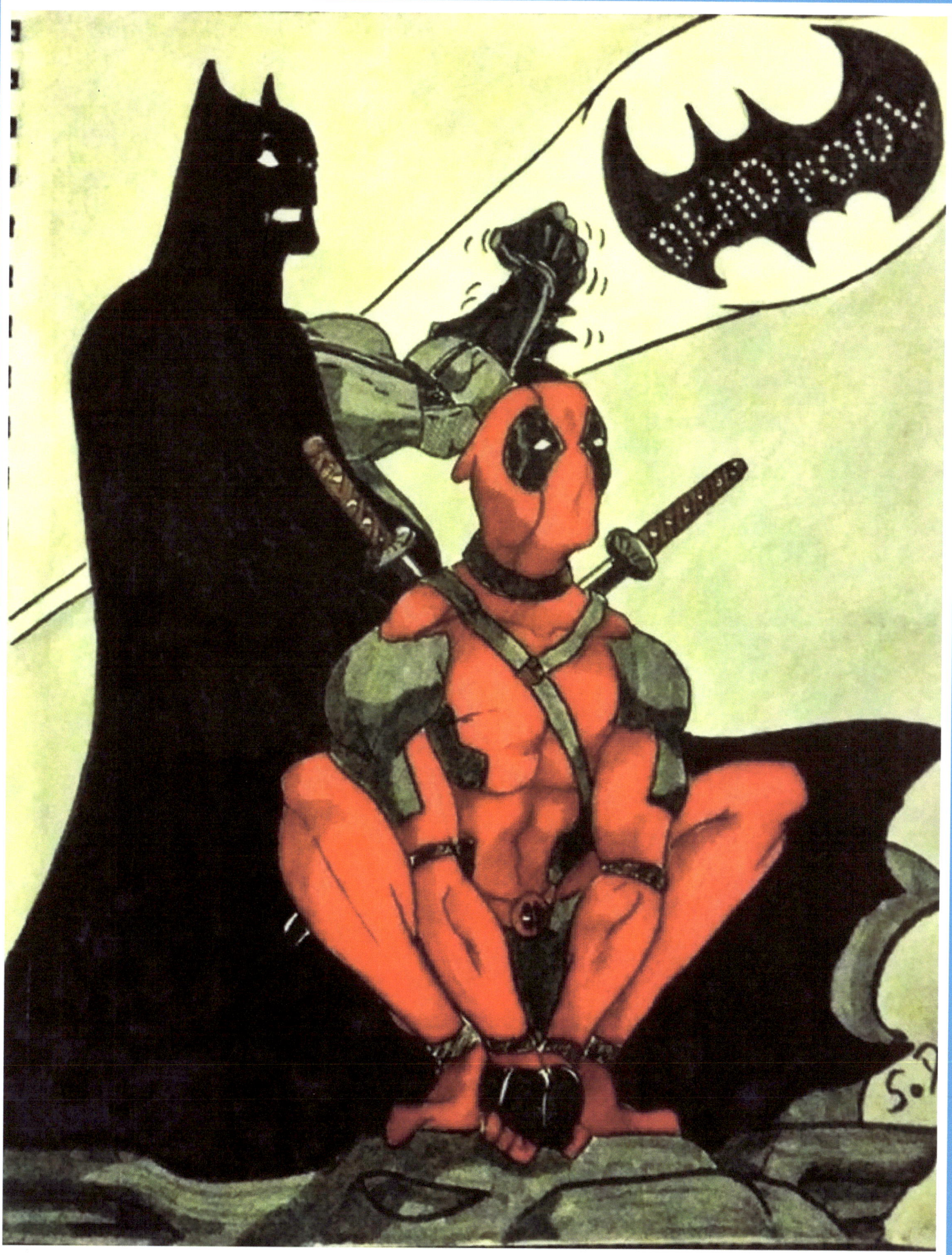

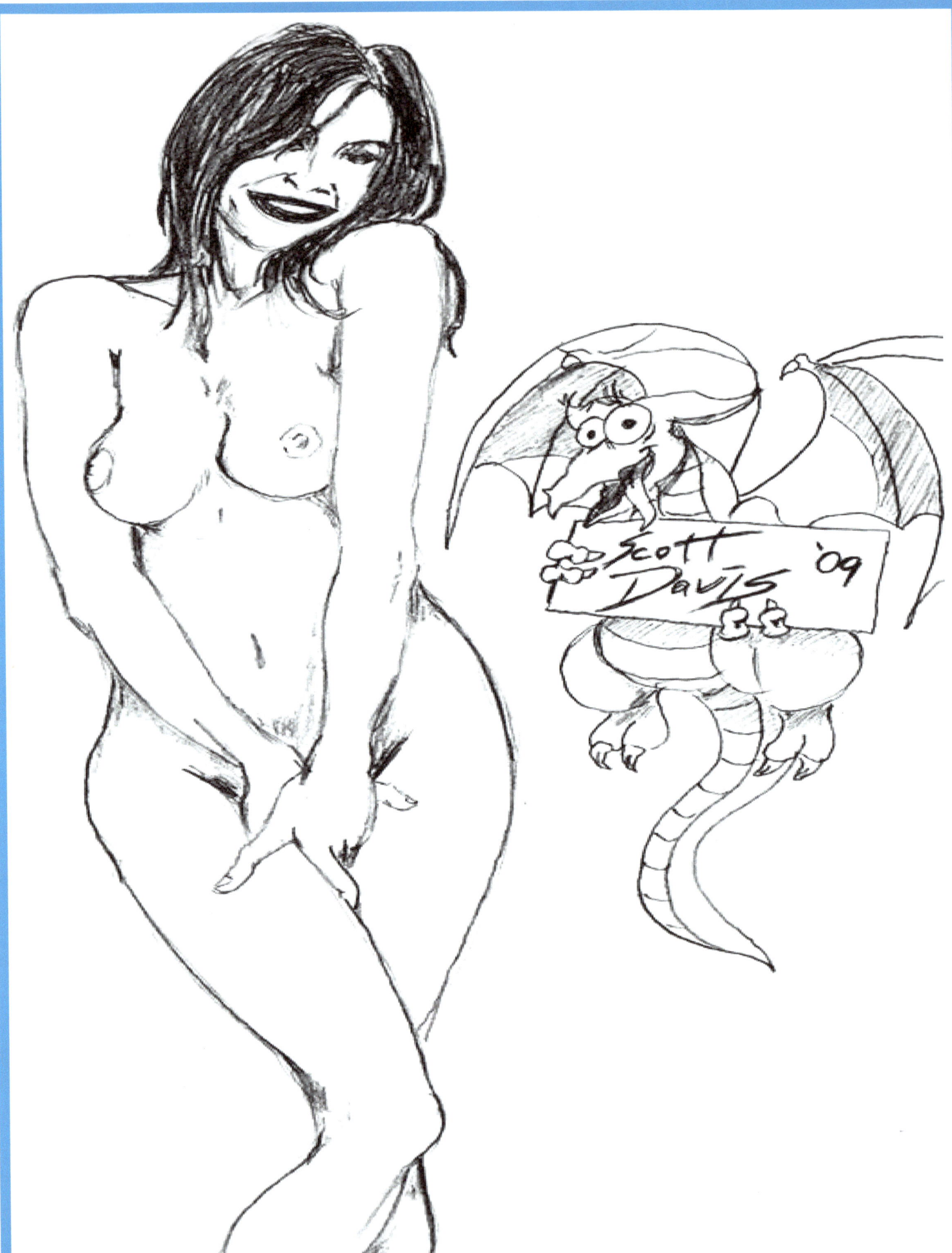

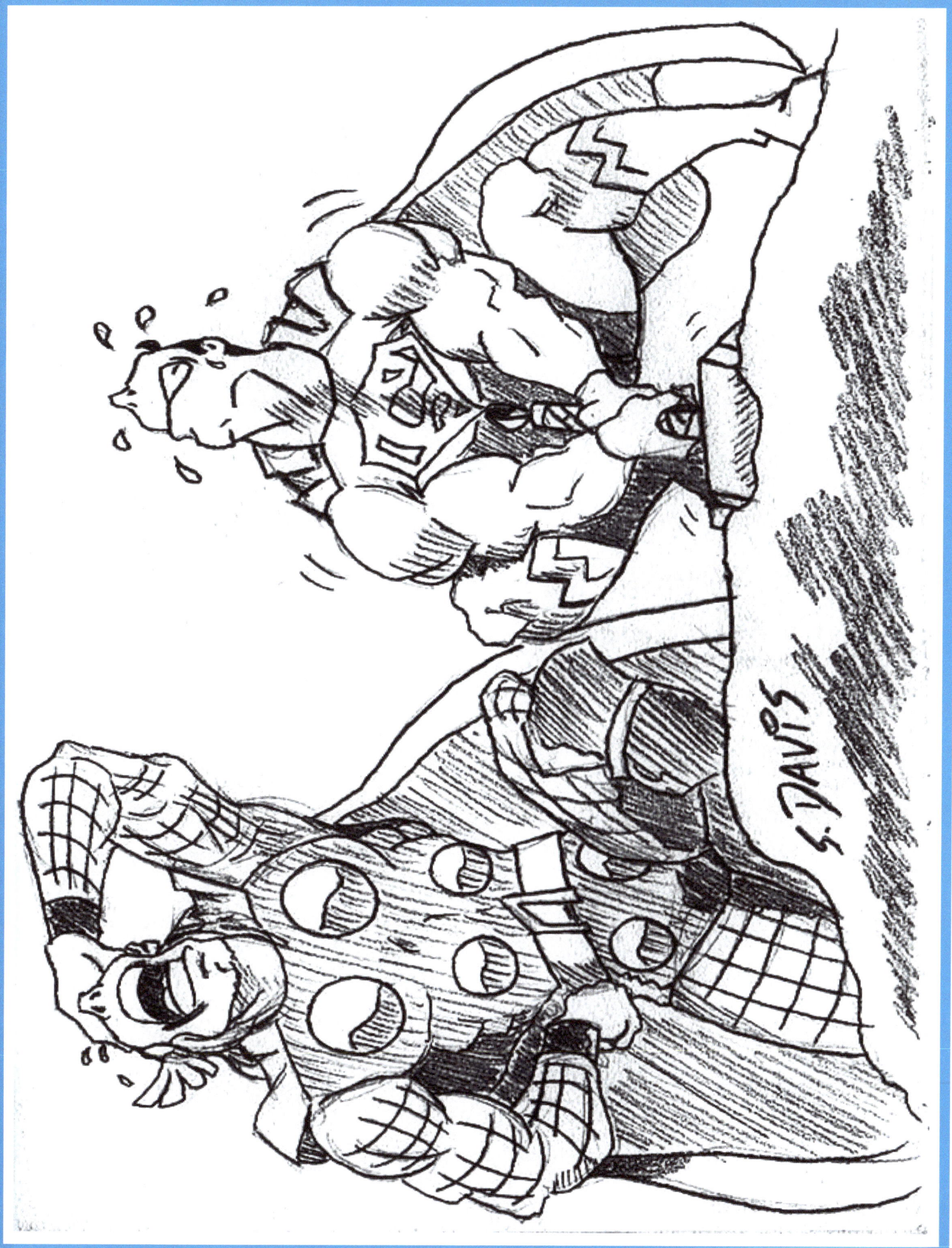

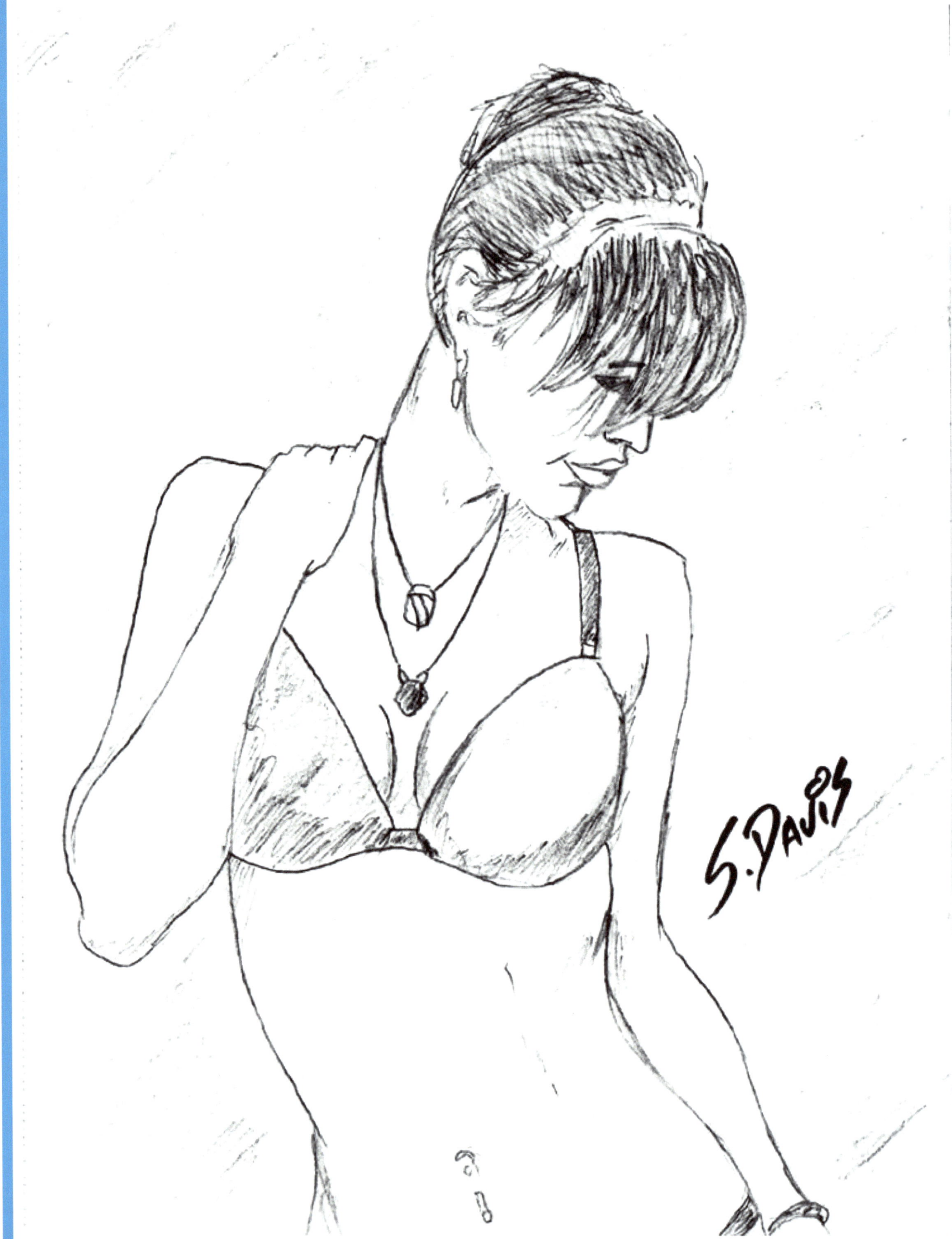

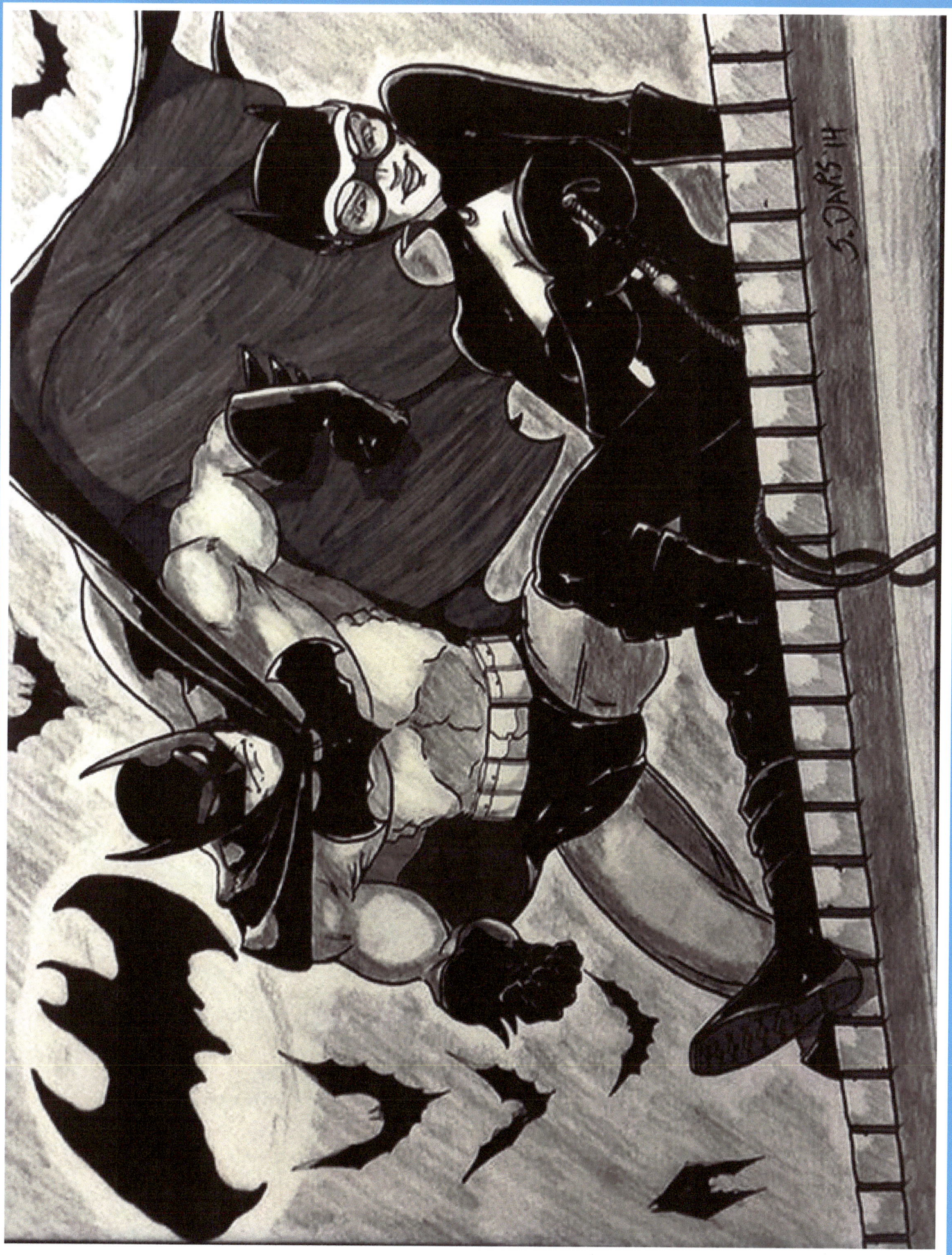

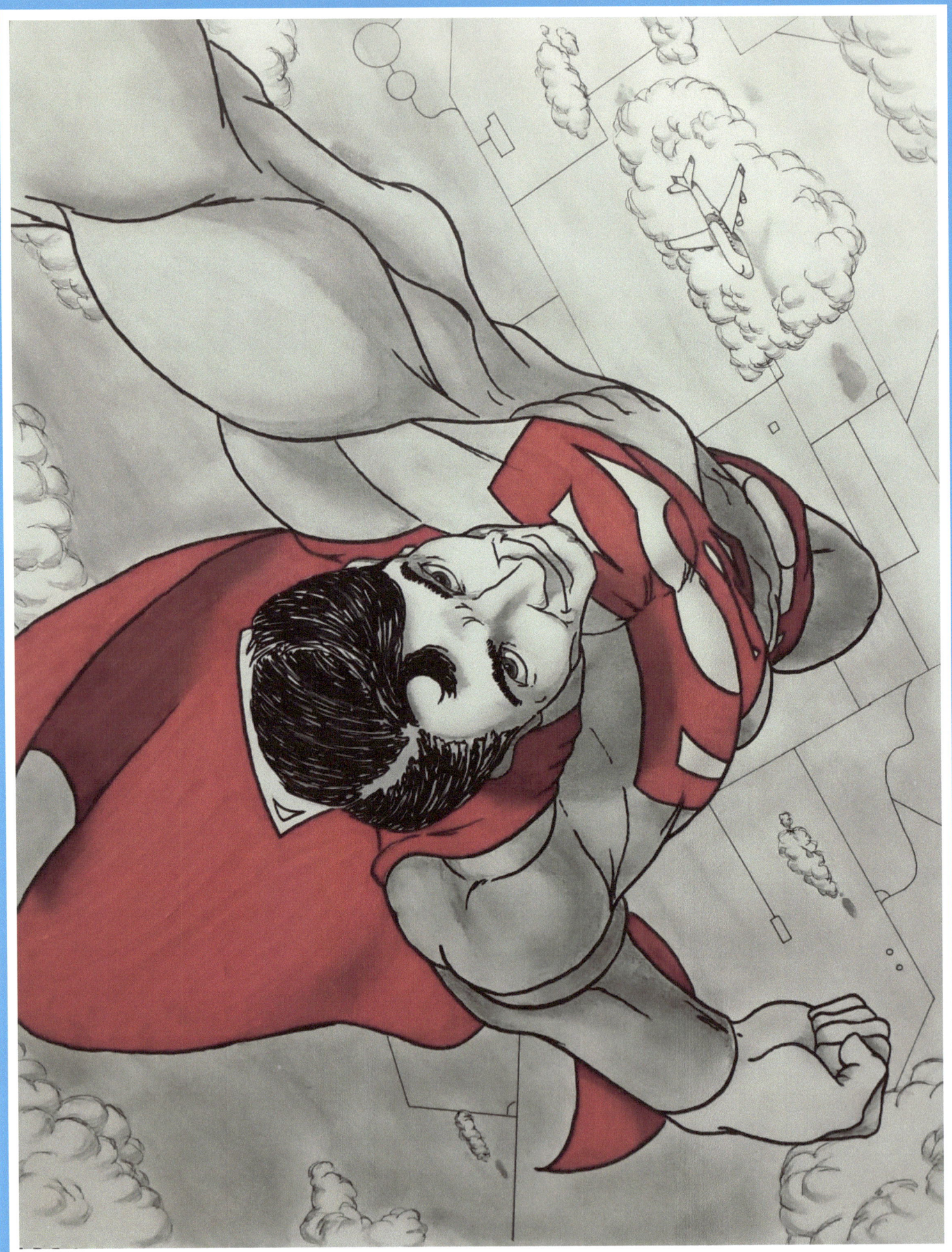

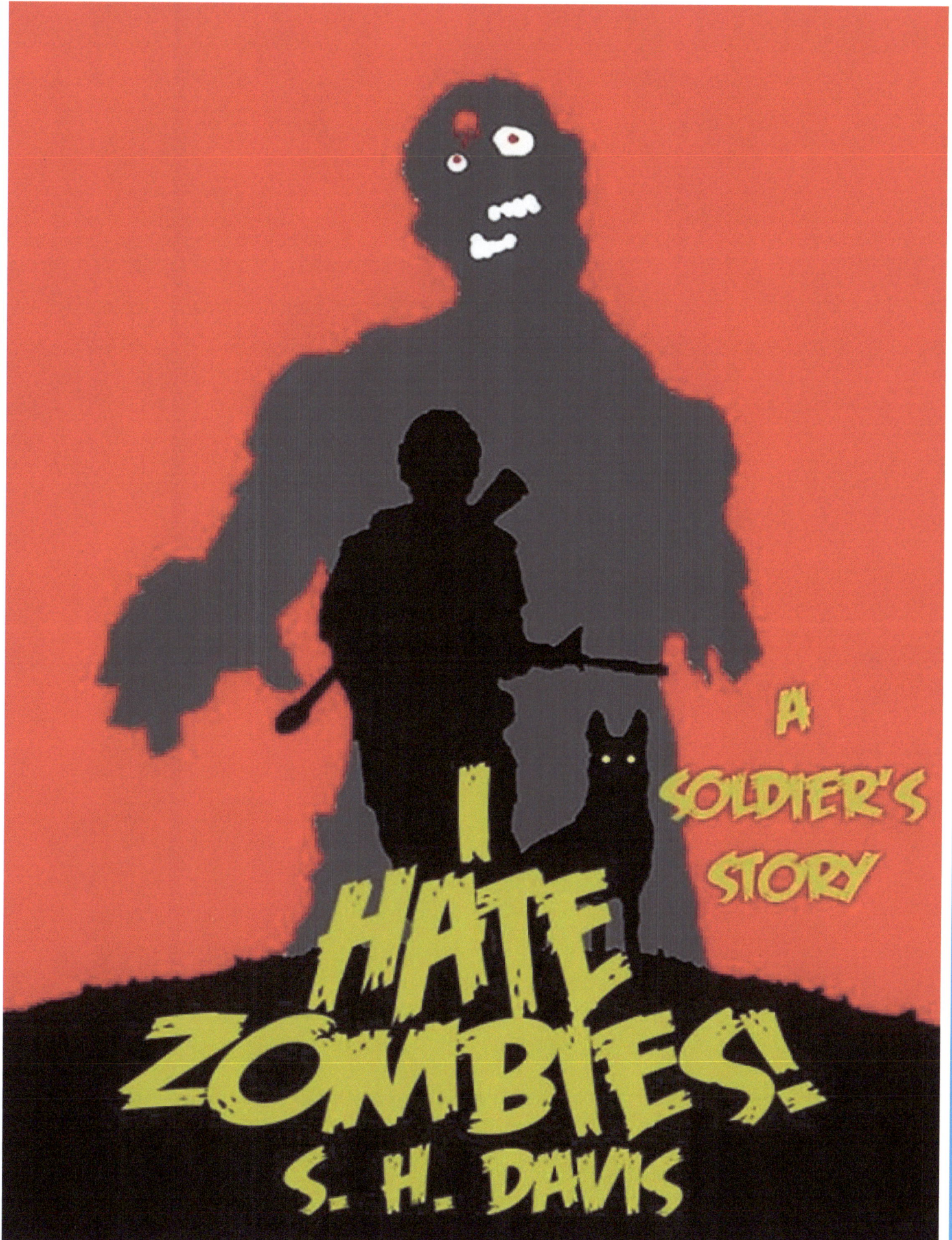

A
SOLDIER'S
STORY

I
HATE
ZOMBIES!
S. H. DAVIS

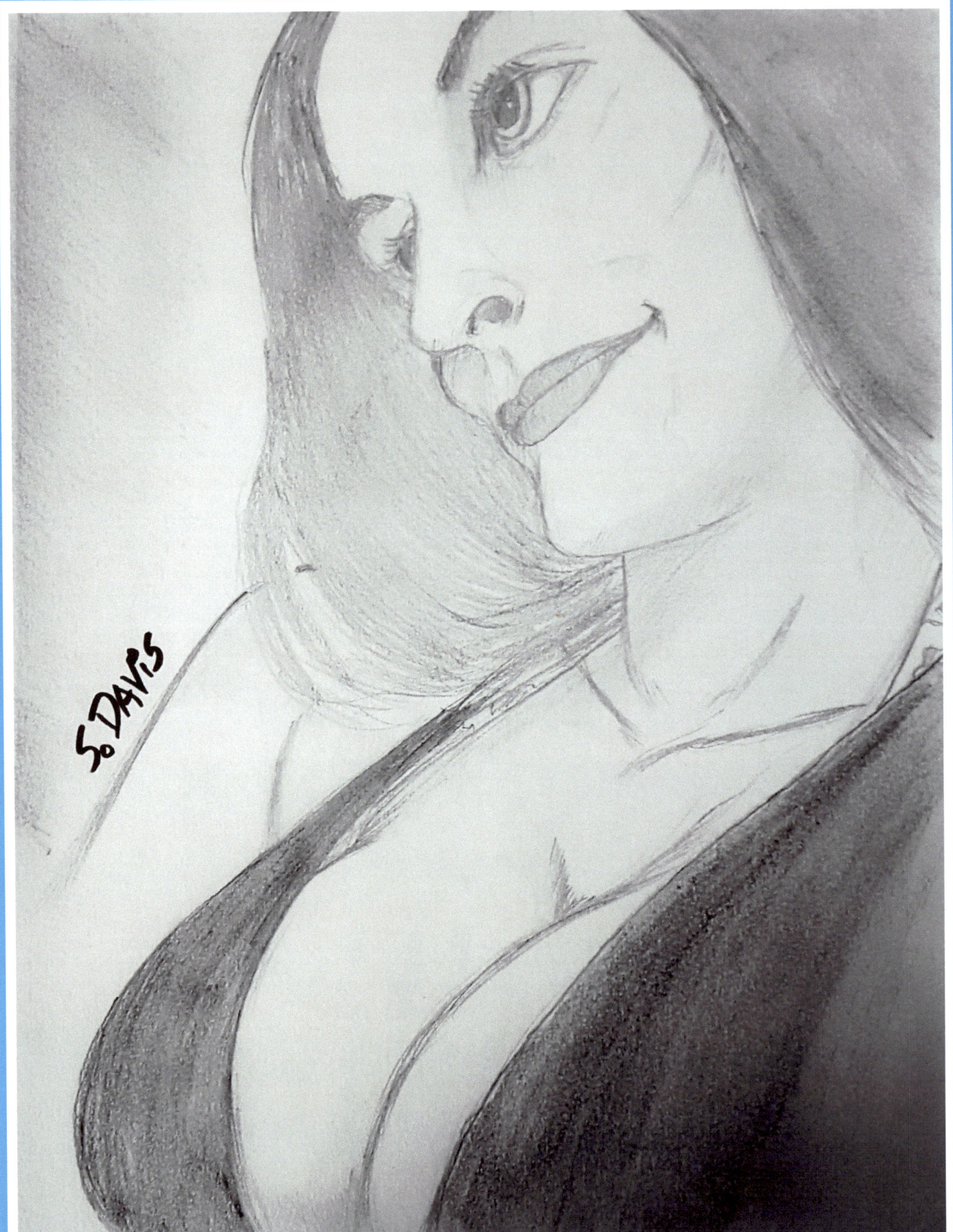

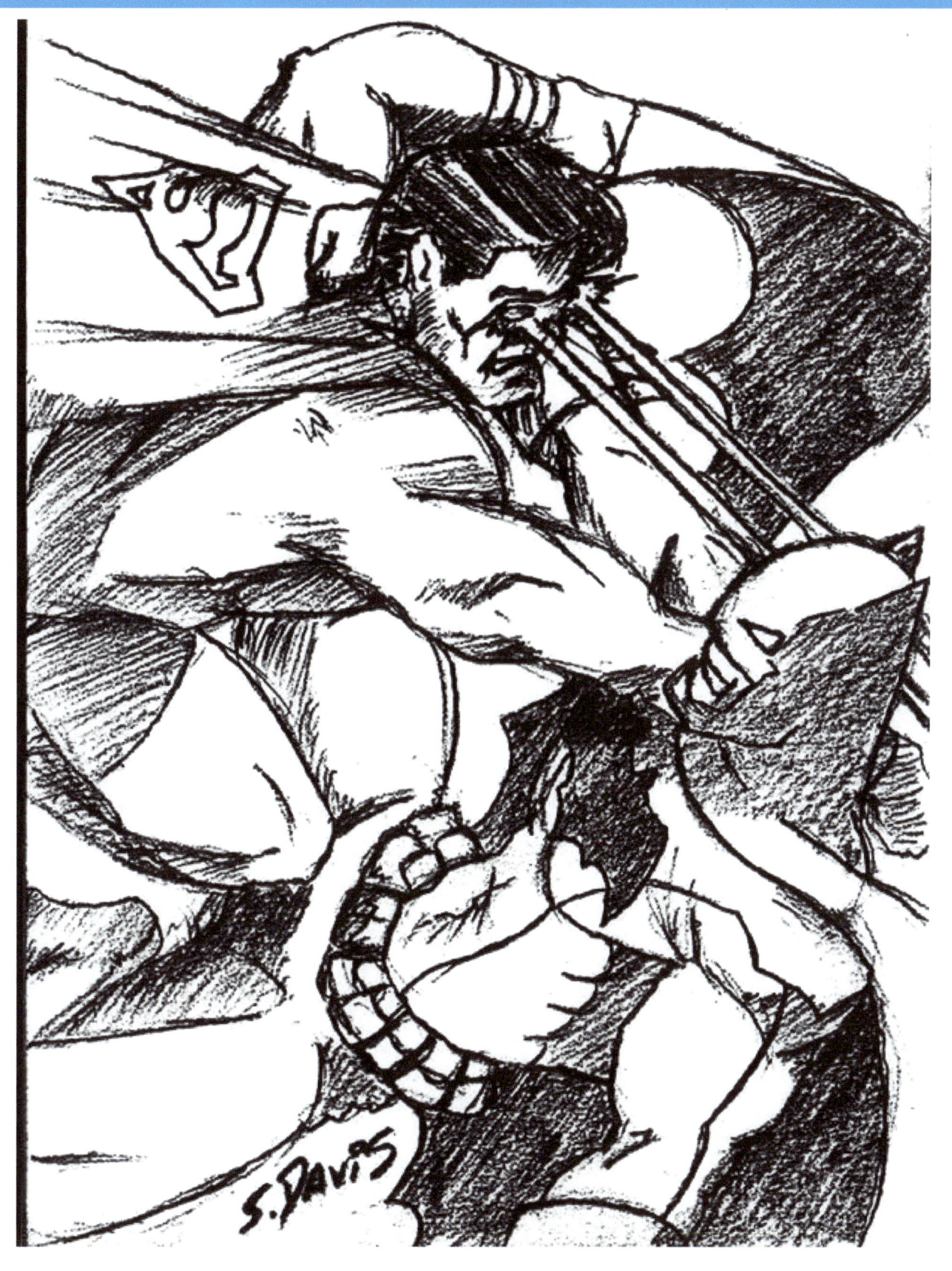

(SPECIAL NOTE: THIS ONE WAS DONE ON A WAFFLE HOUSE SCRAP
PIECE OF PAPER 5X6)

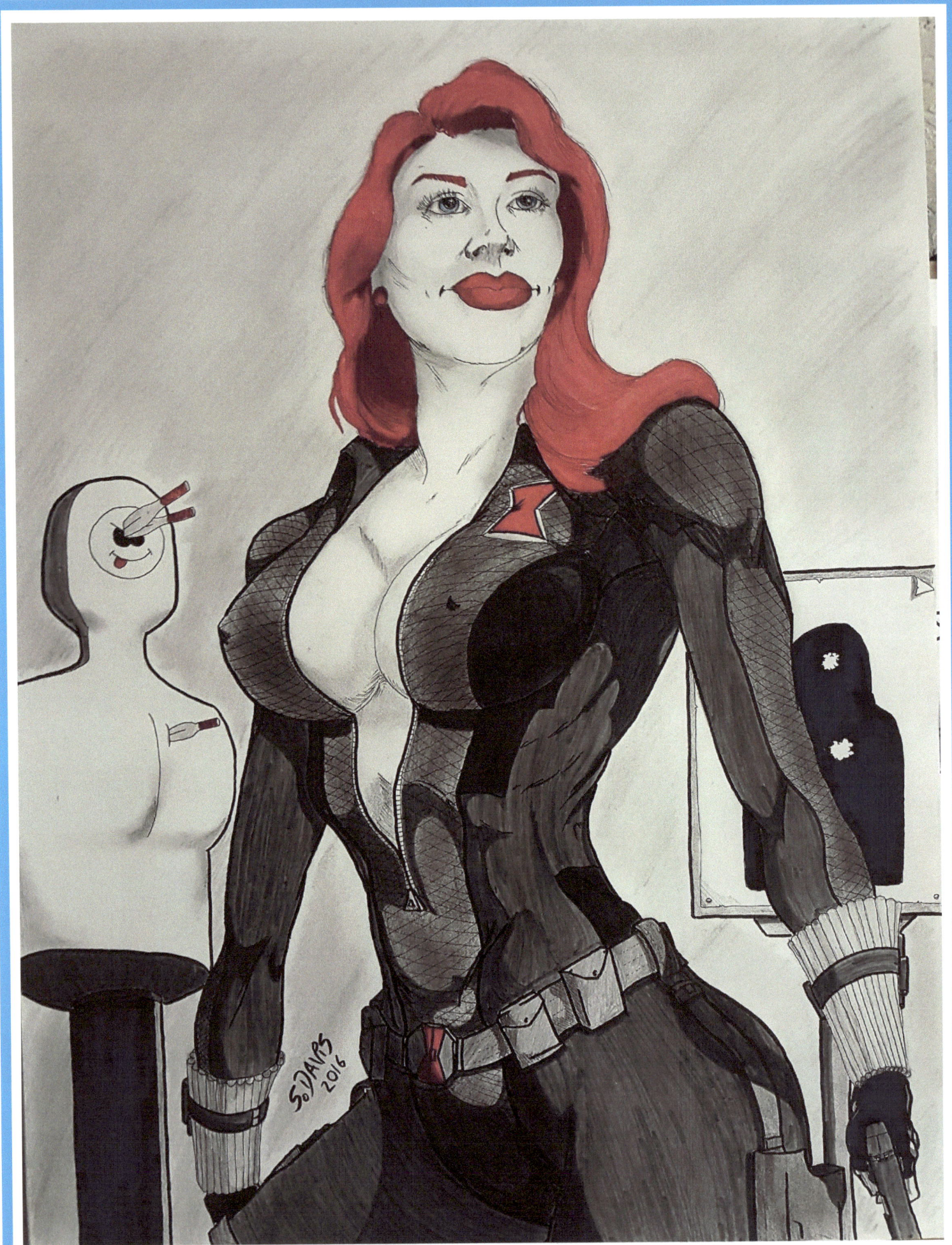

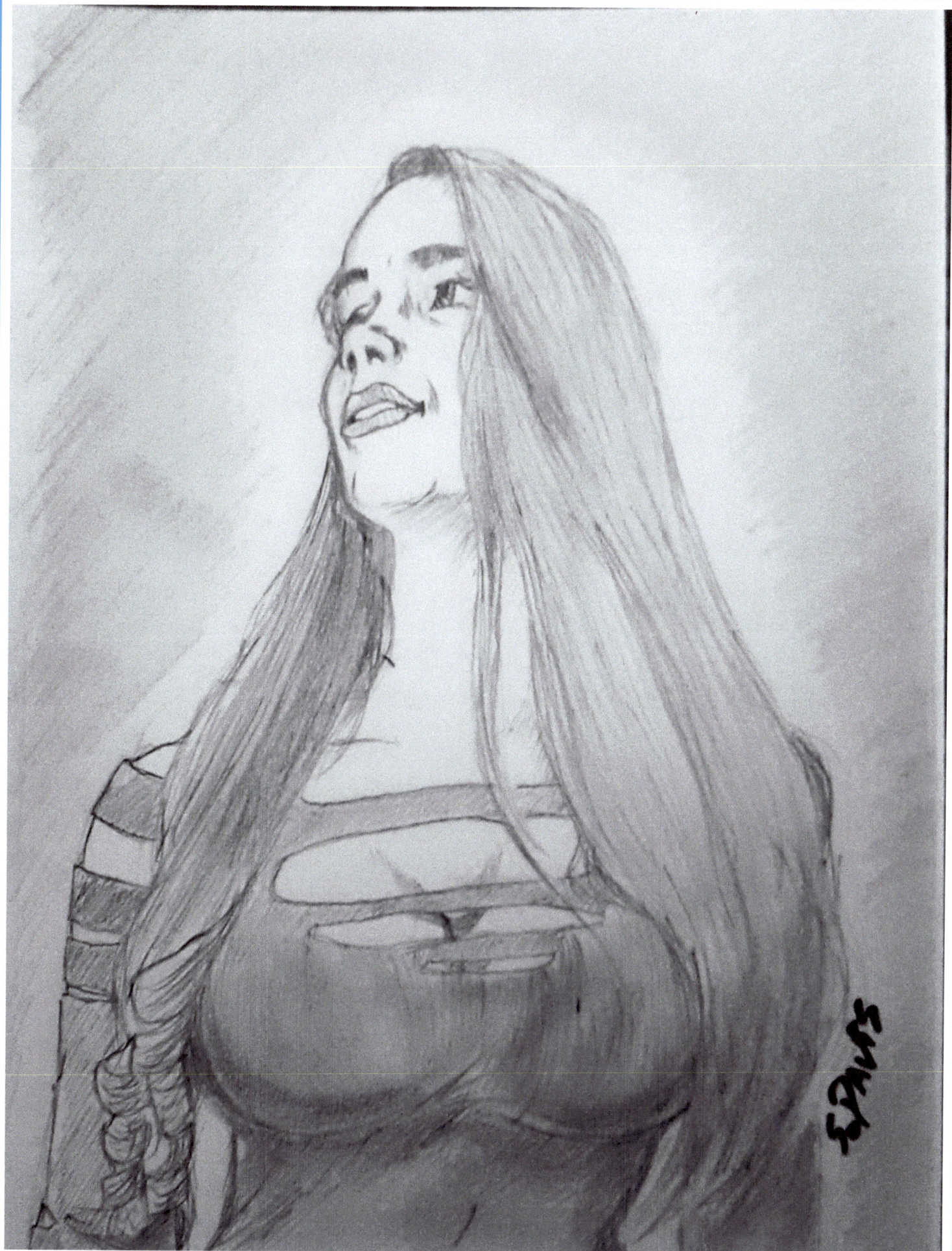

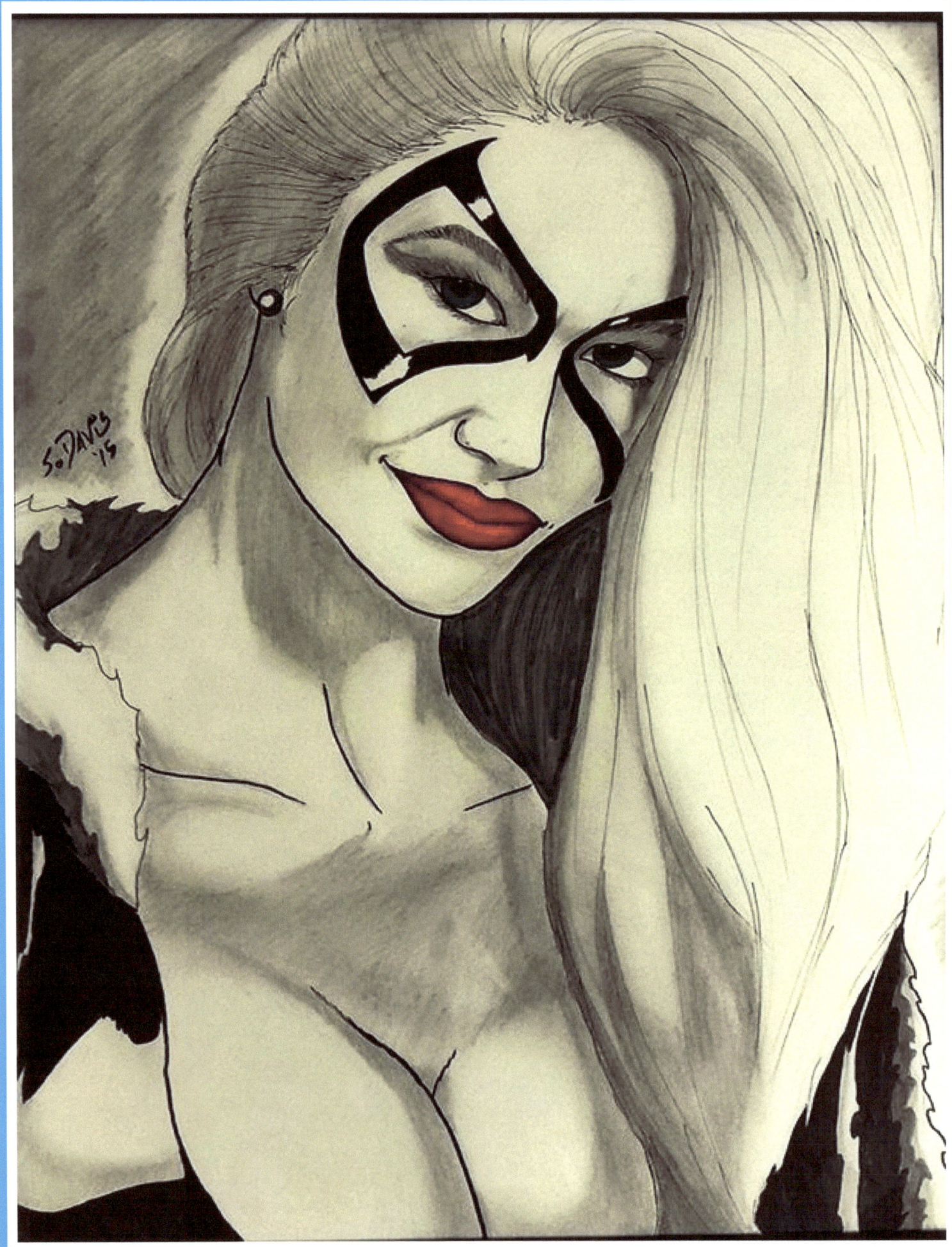

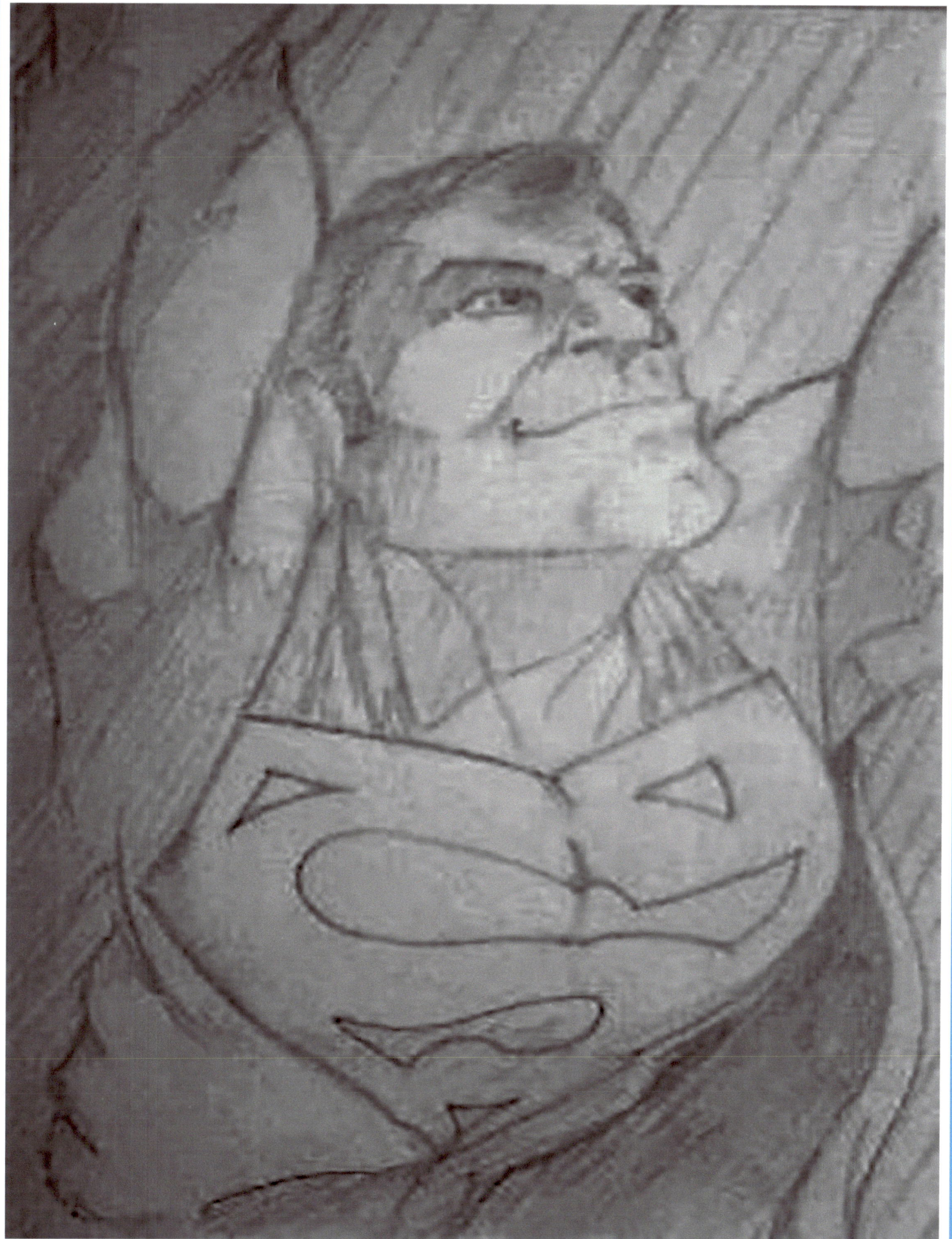

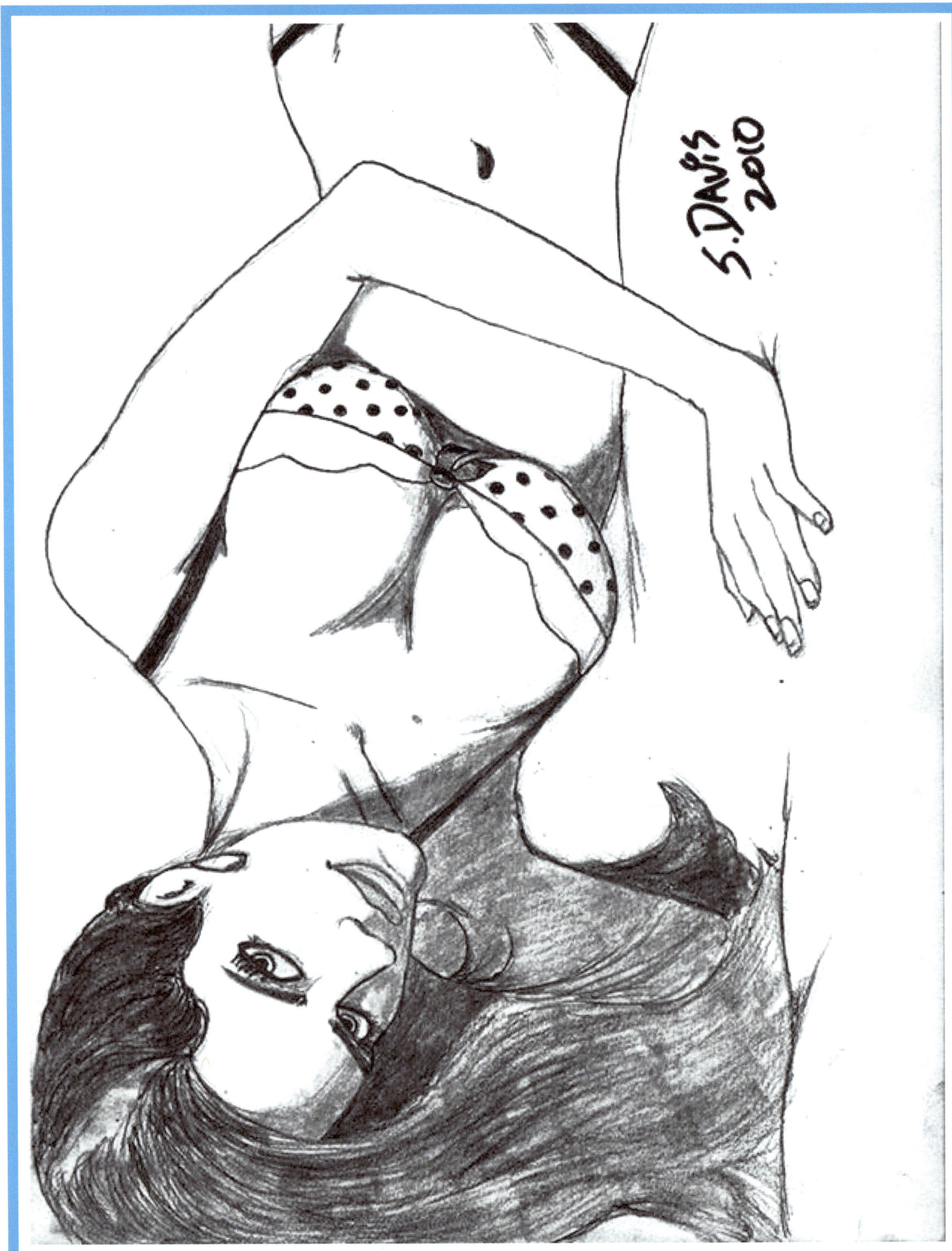

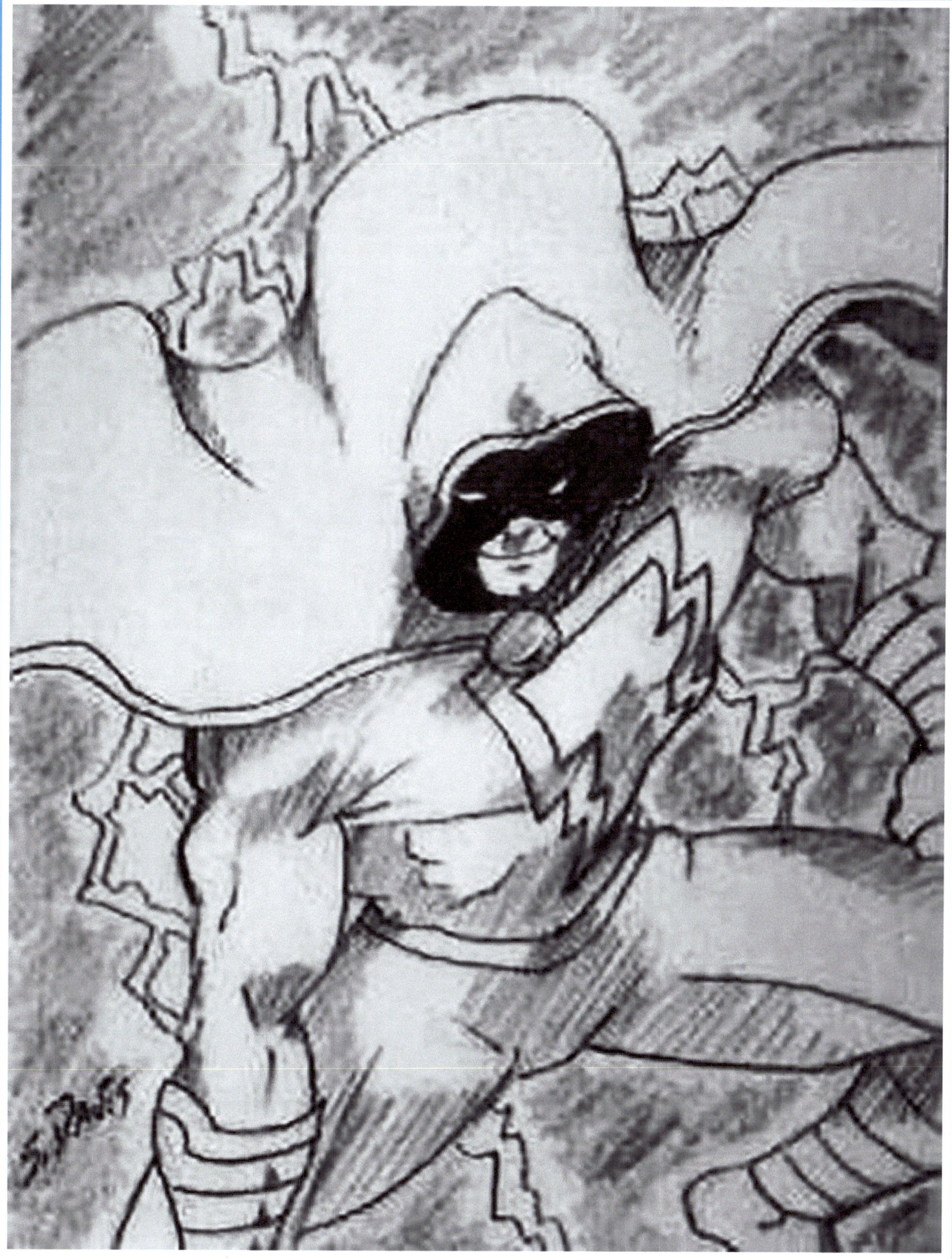

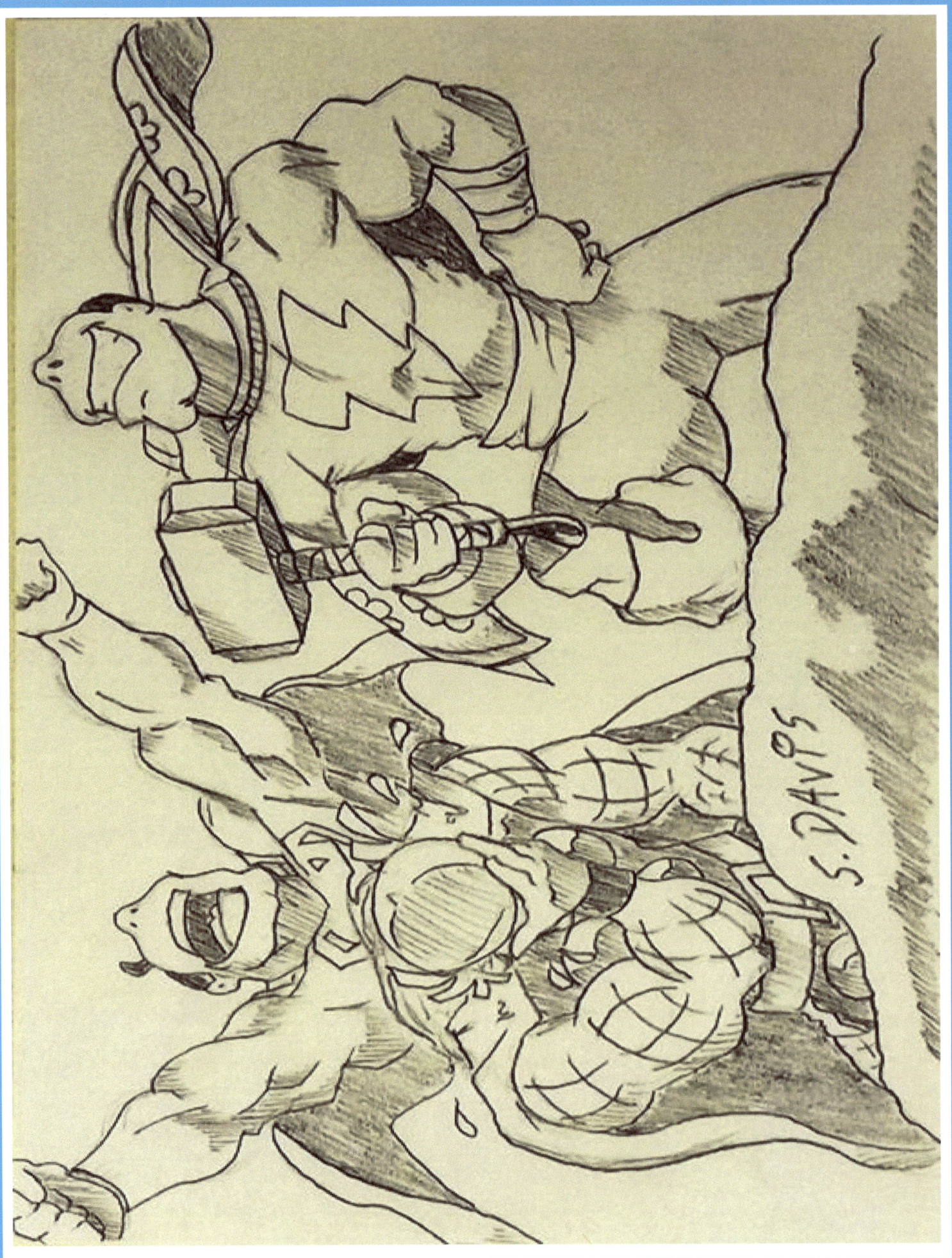

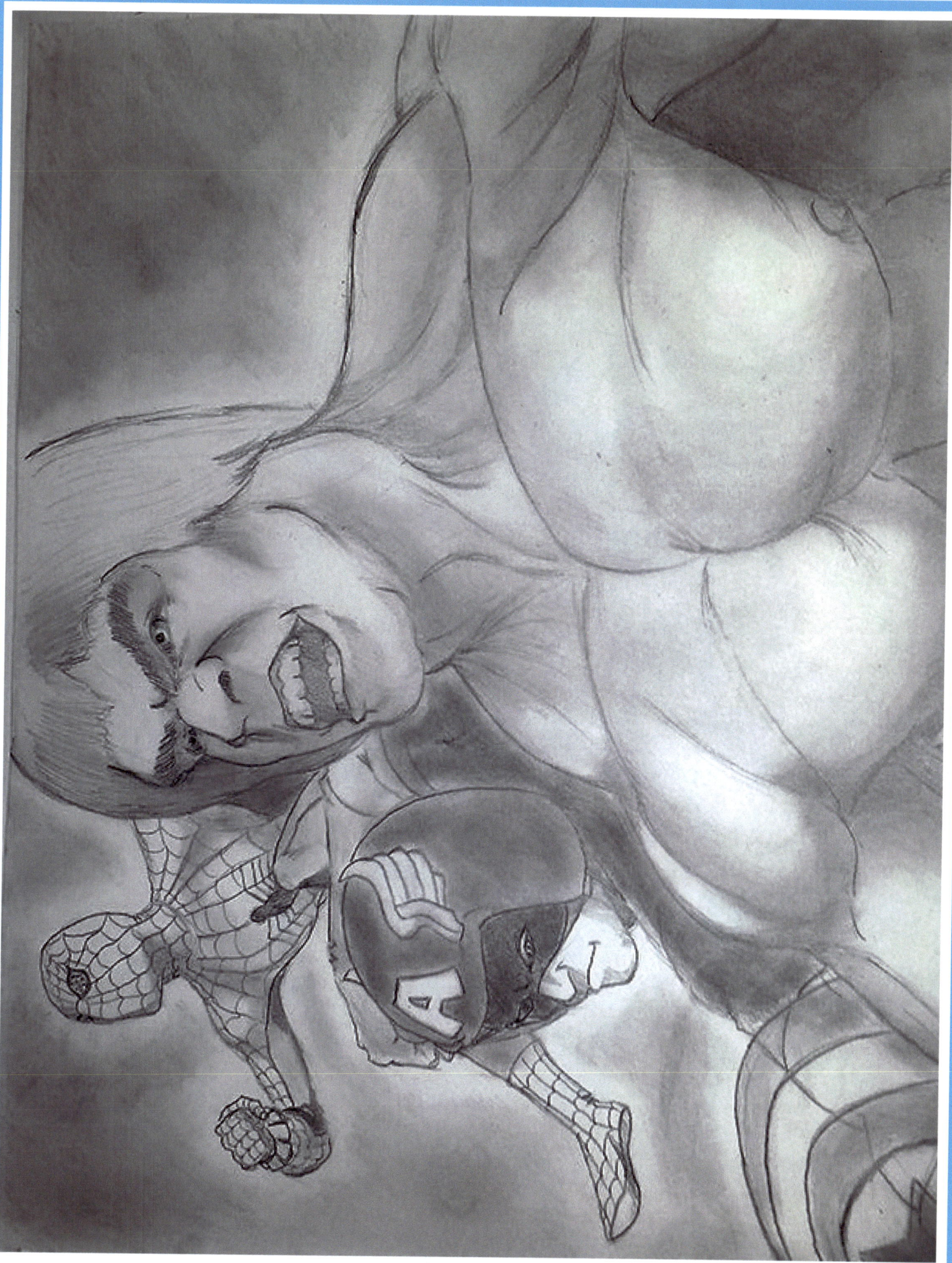

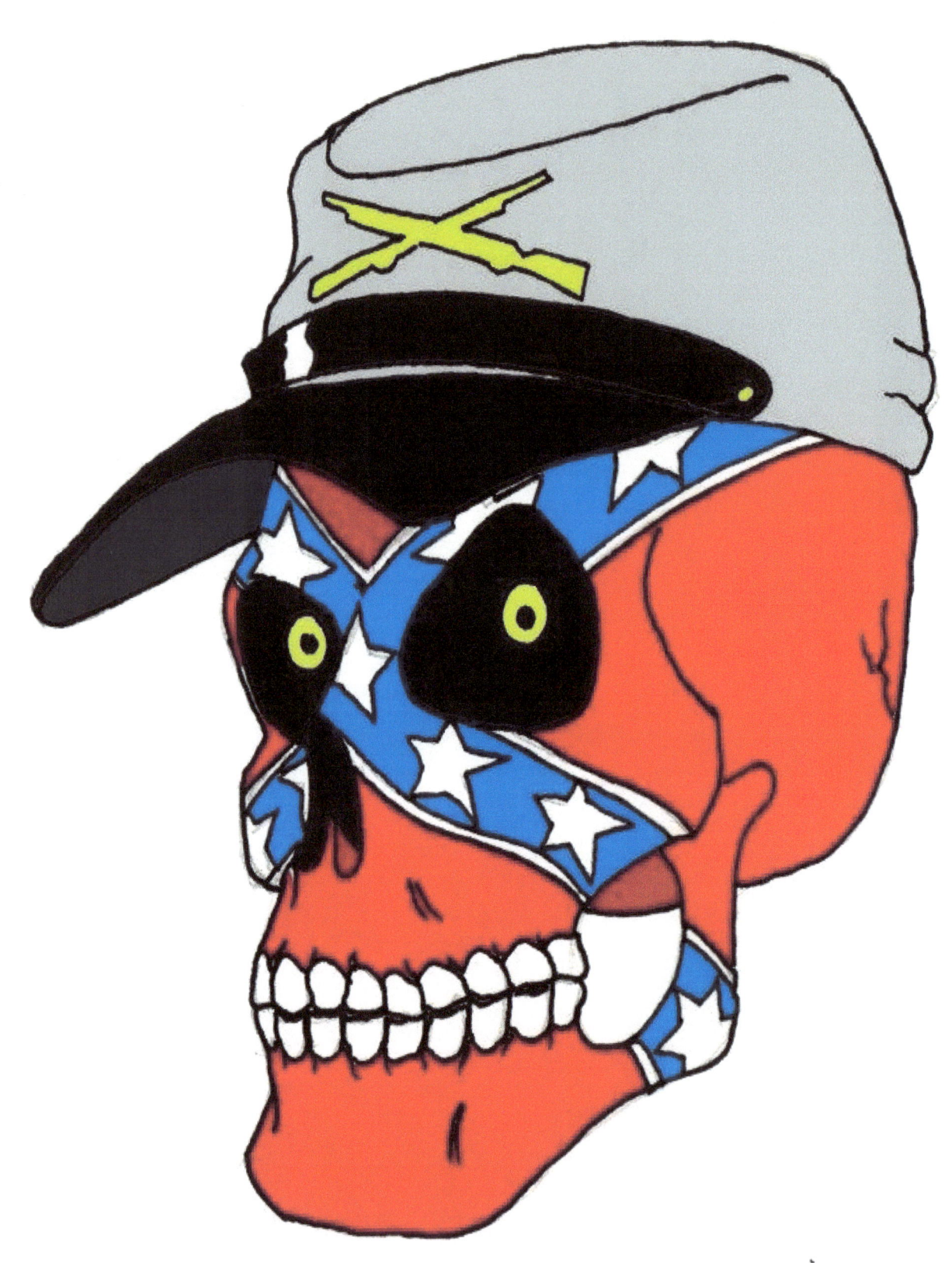

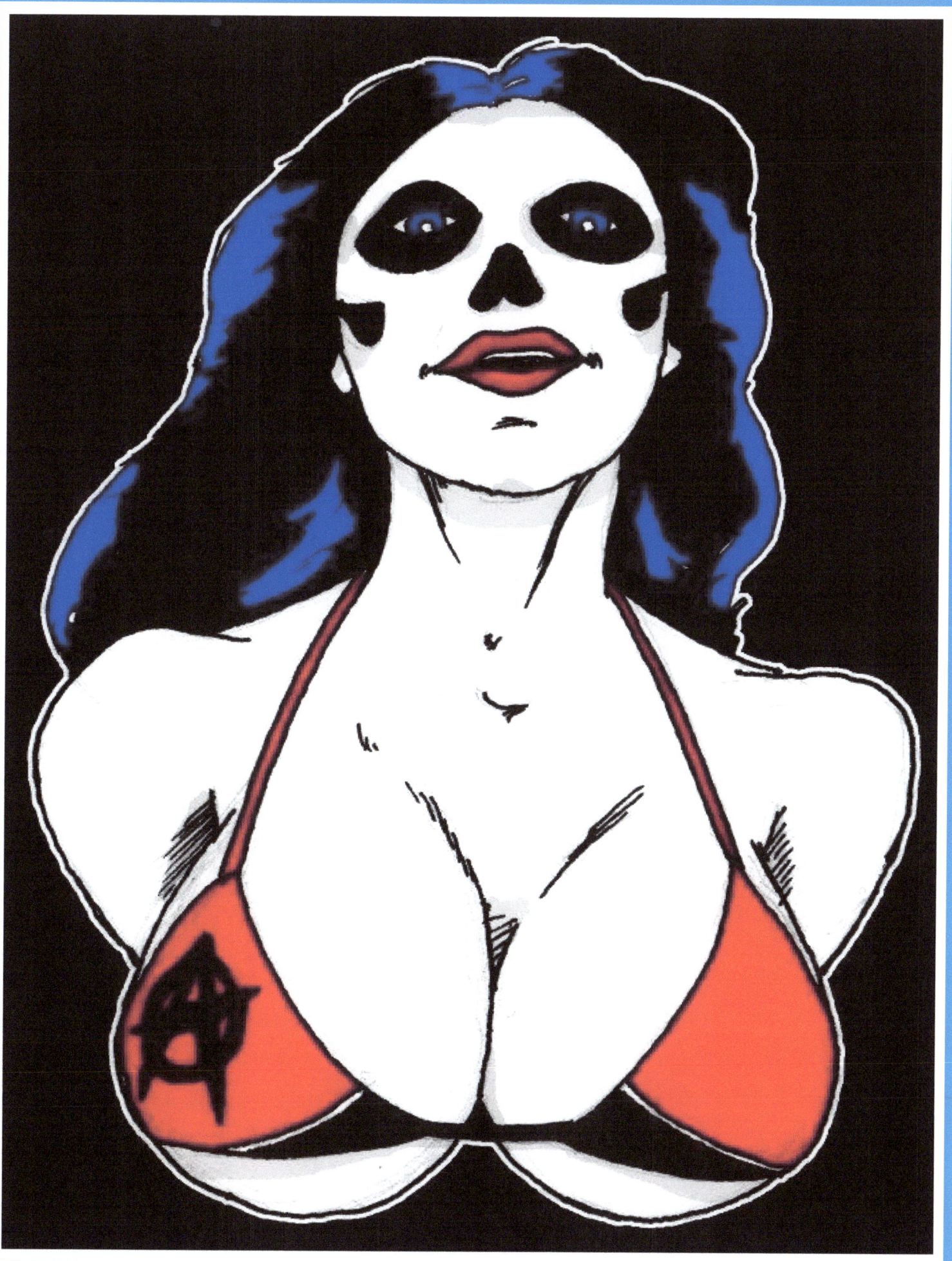

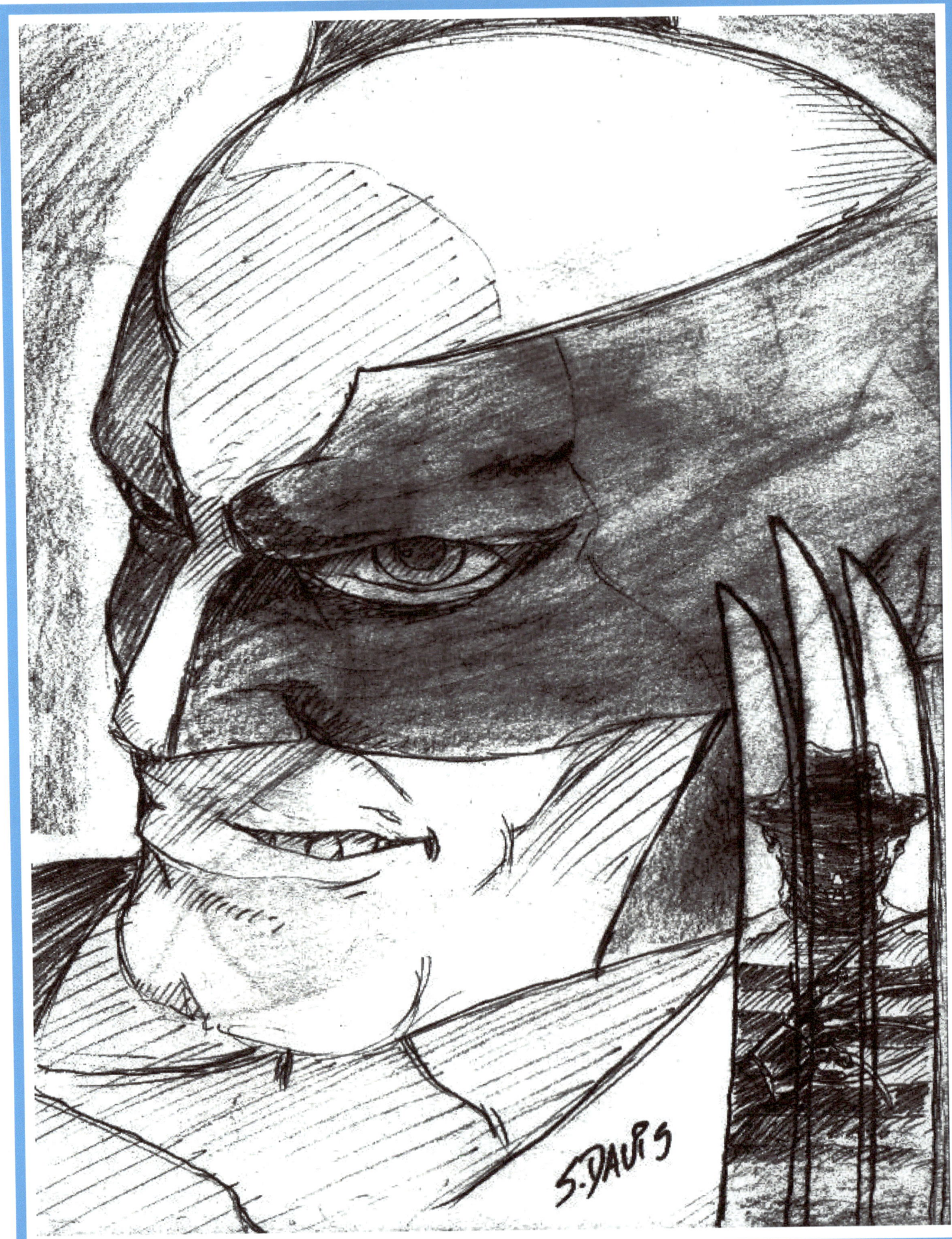

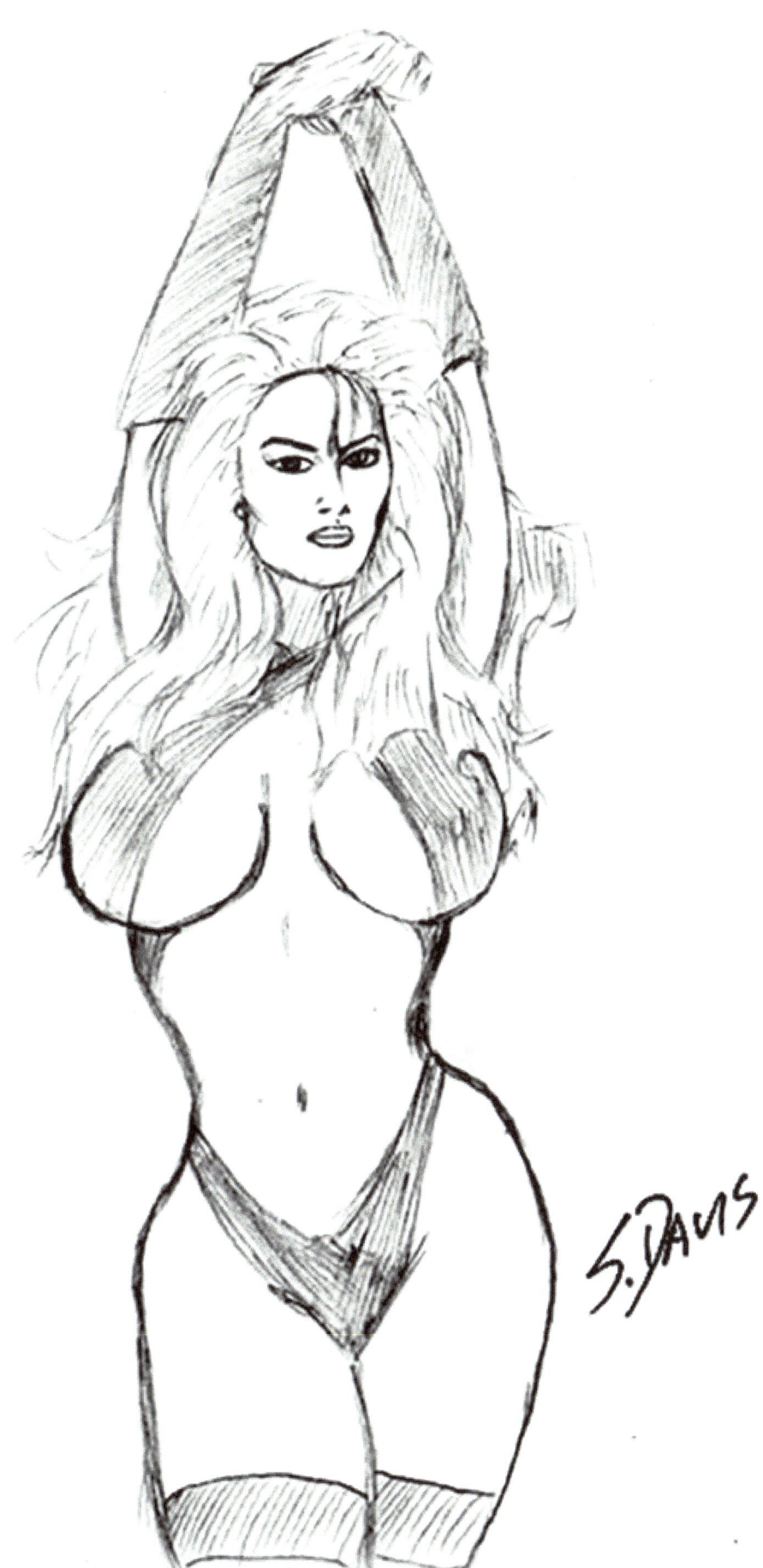

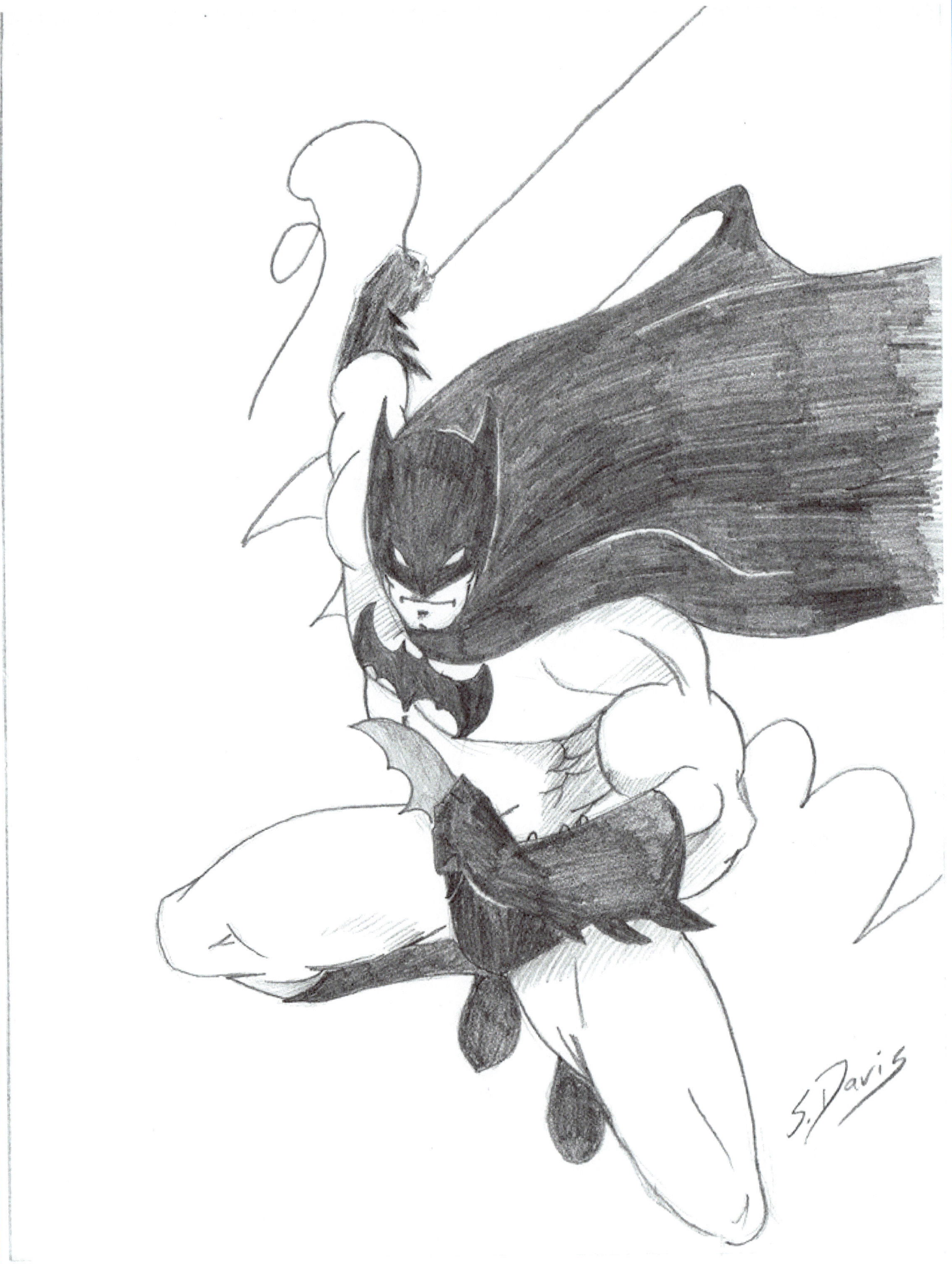

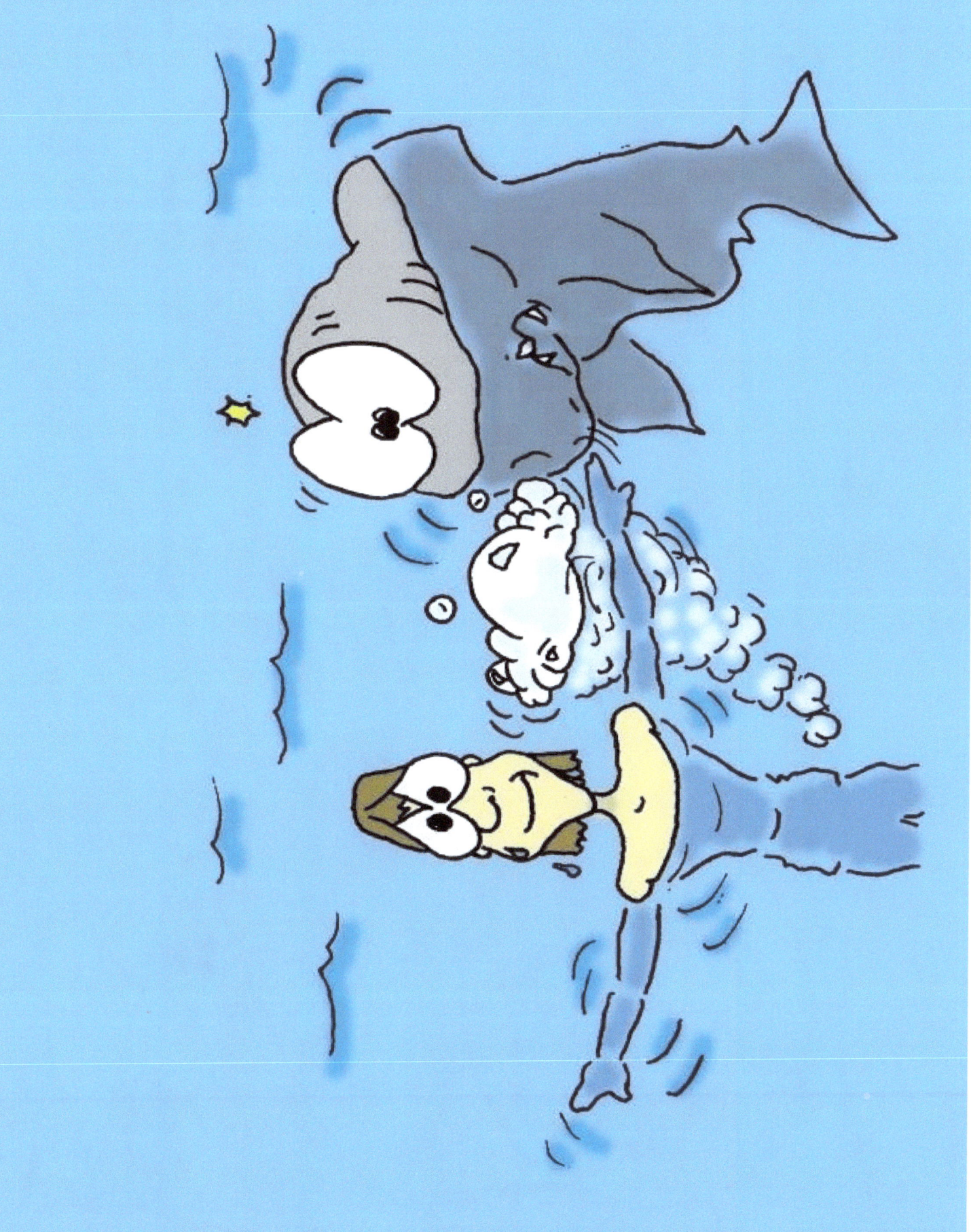

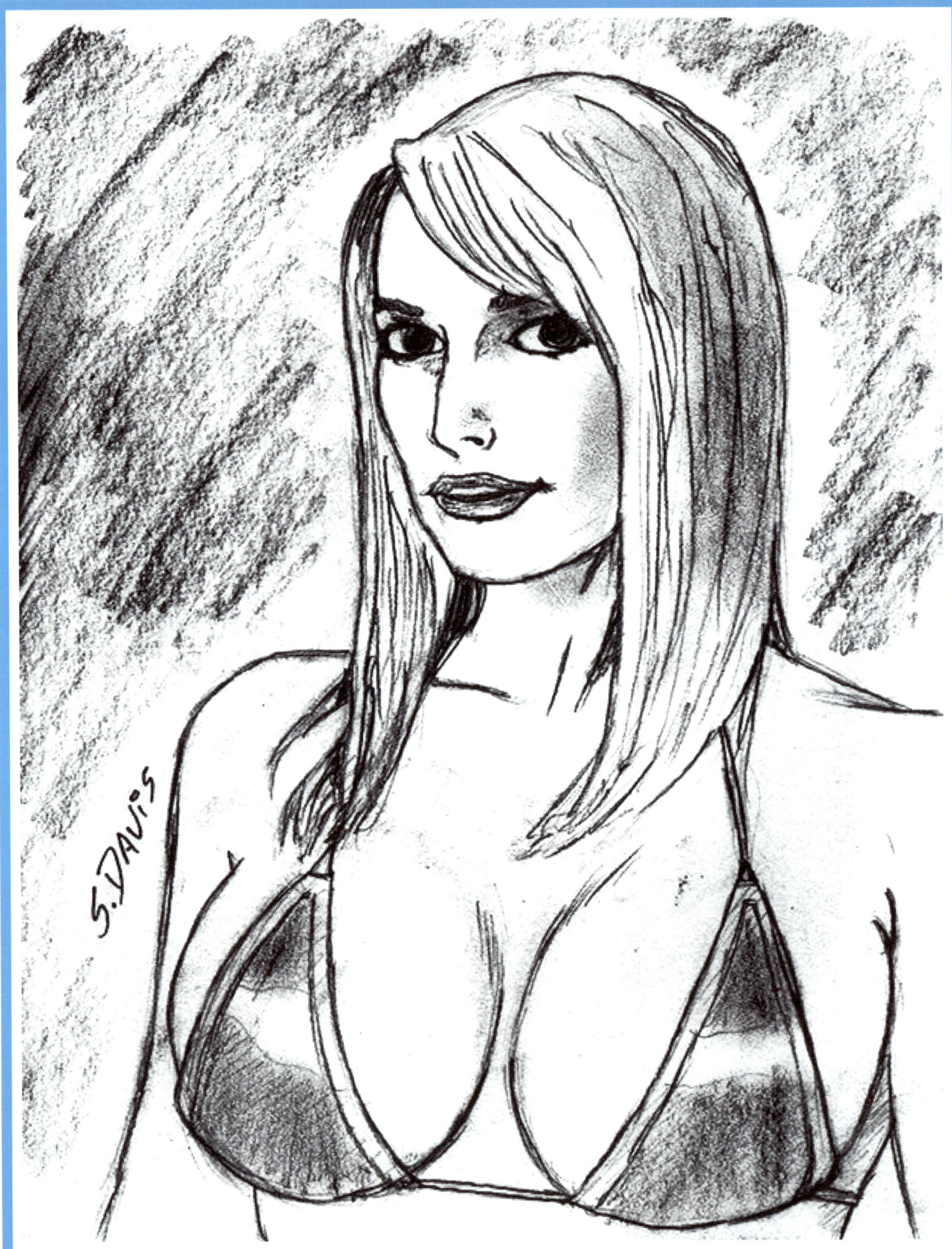

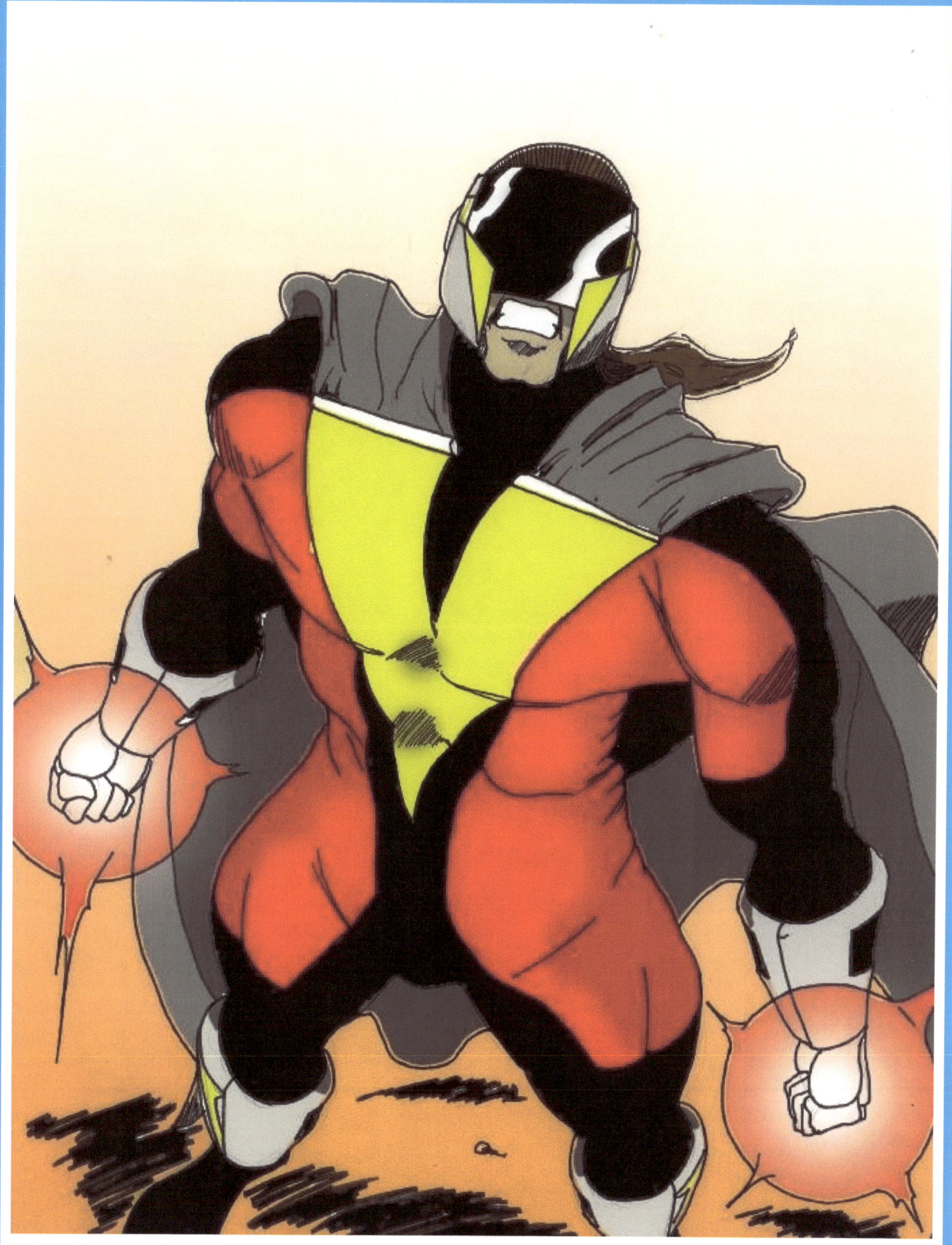

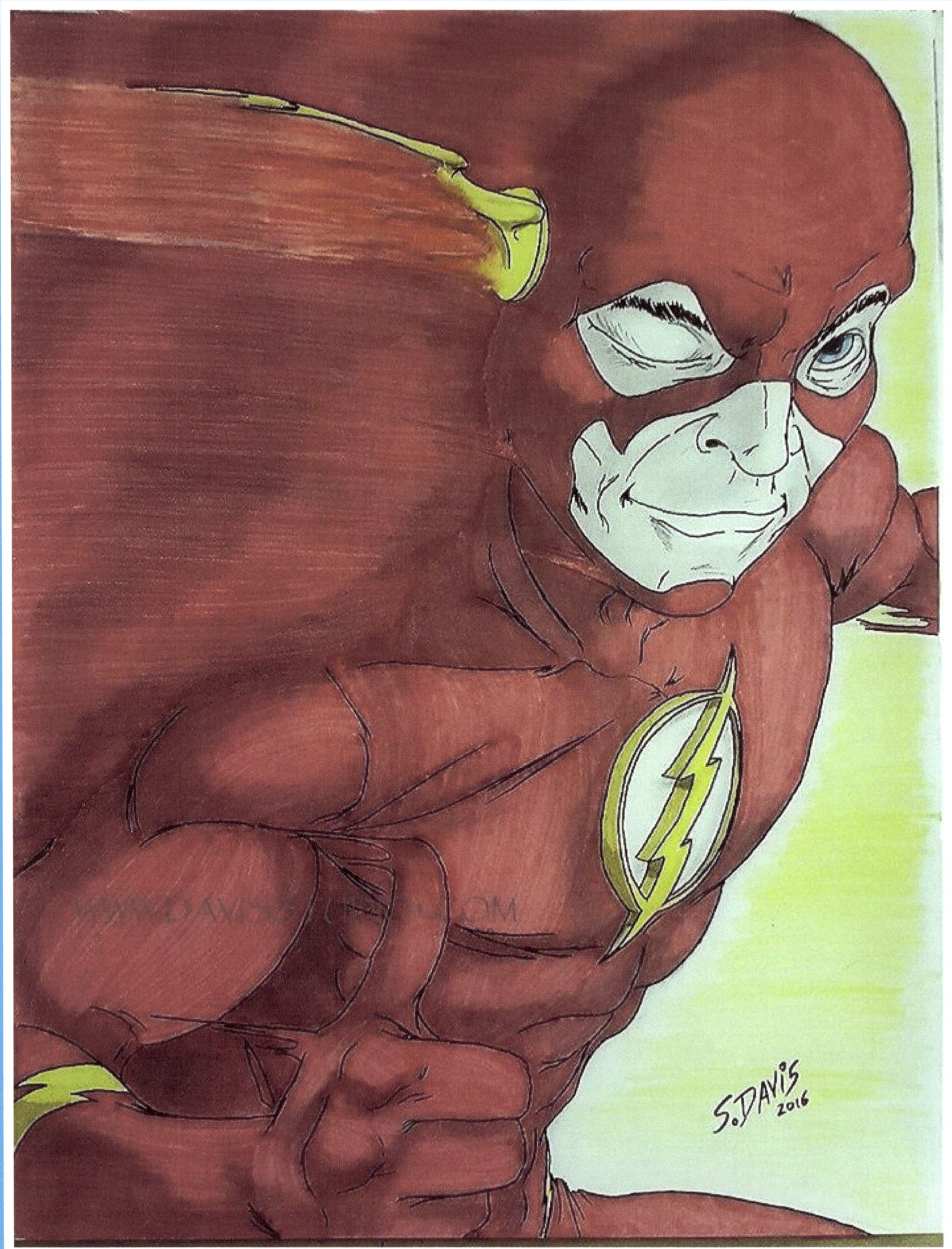

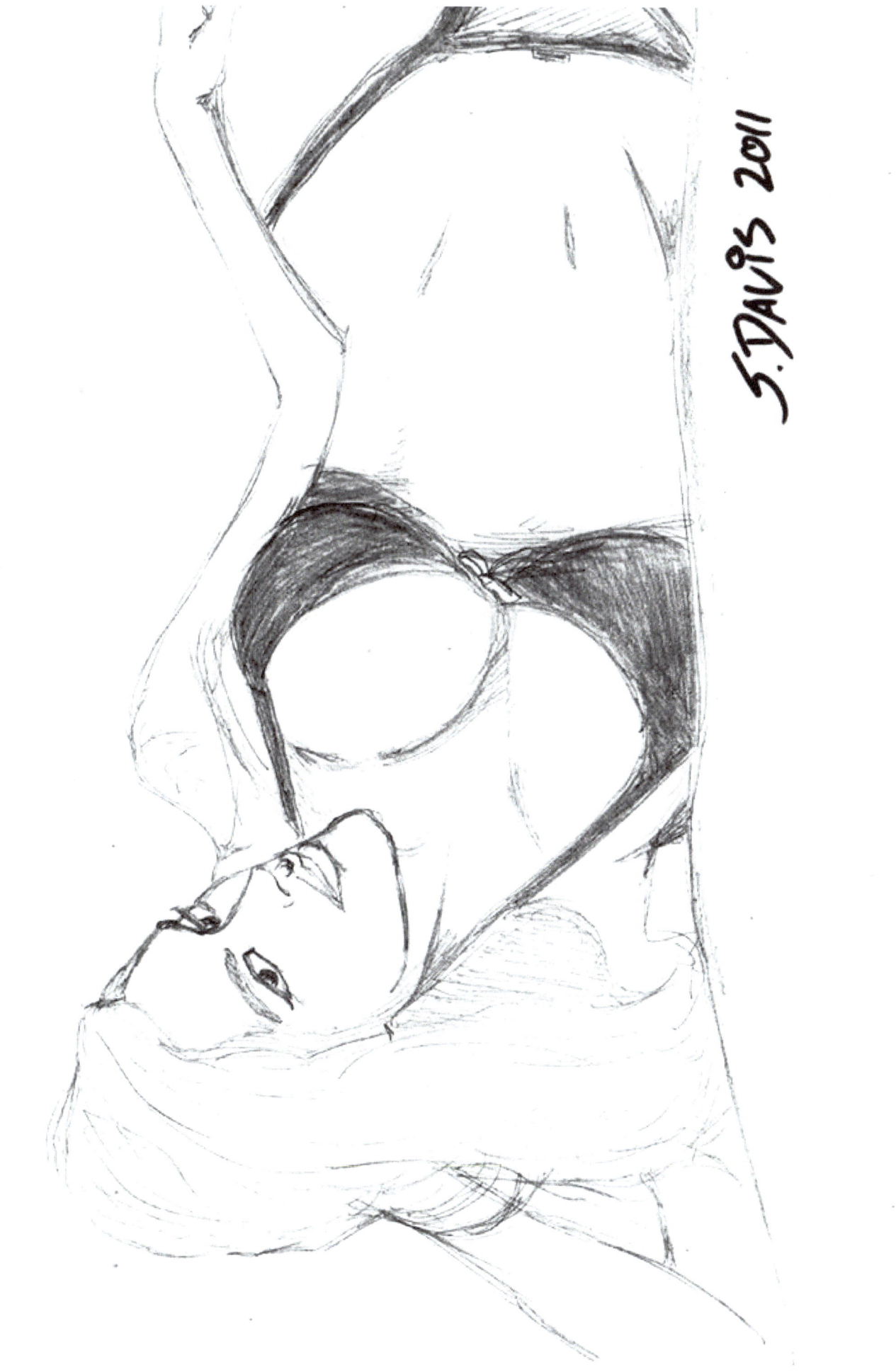

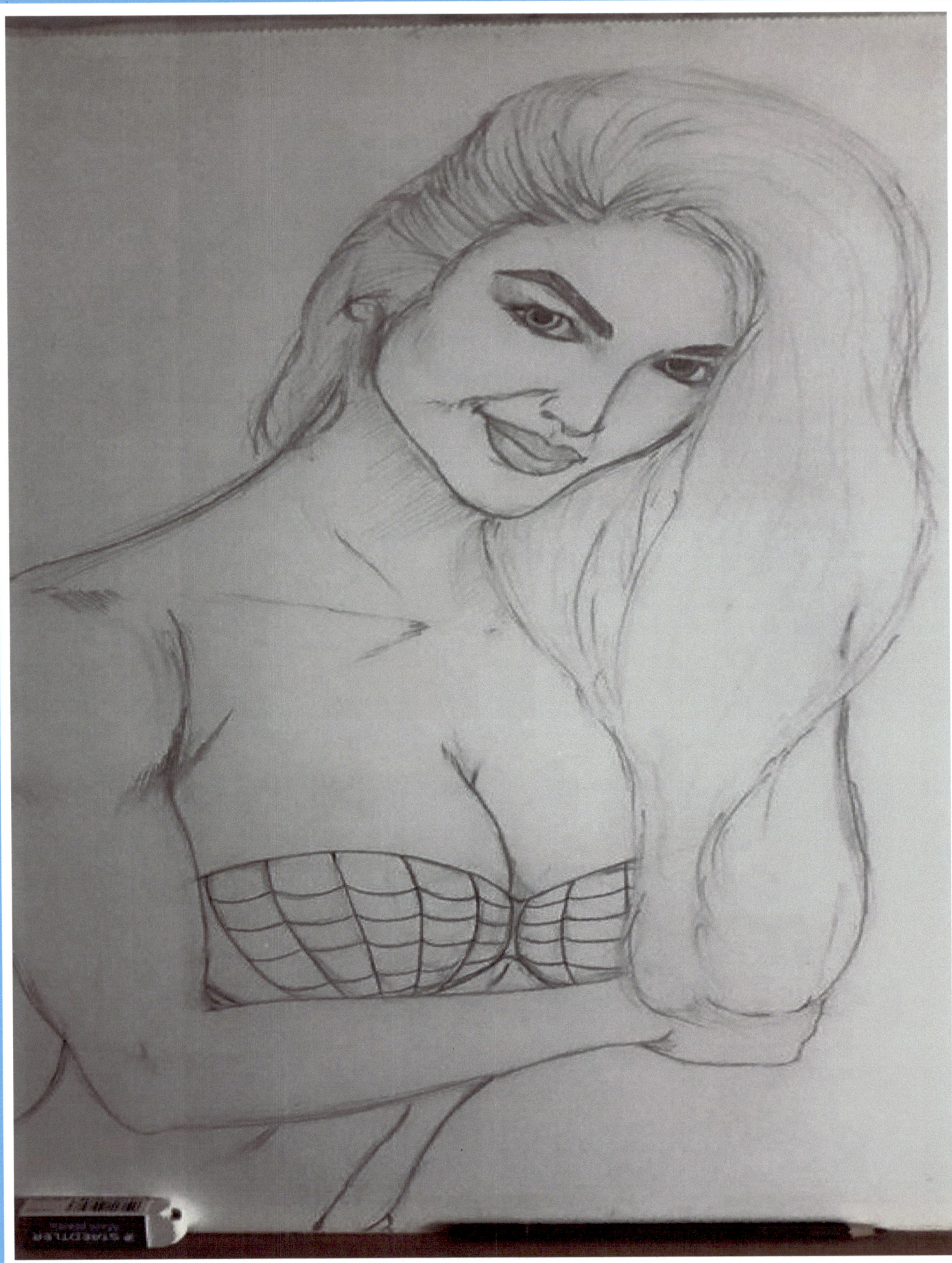

# WAR WOLF

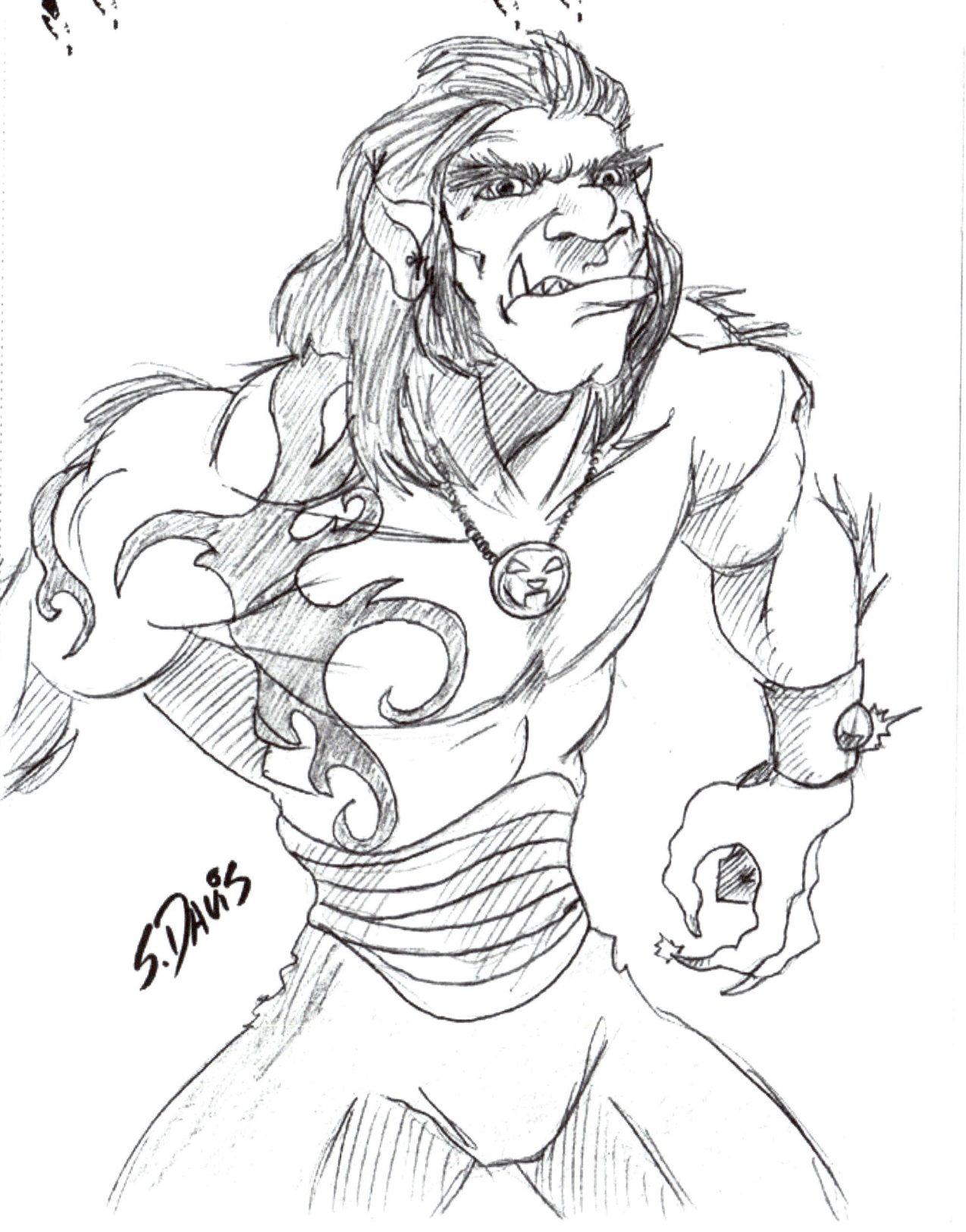

S. Davis

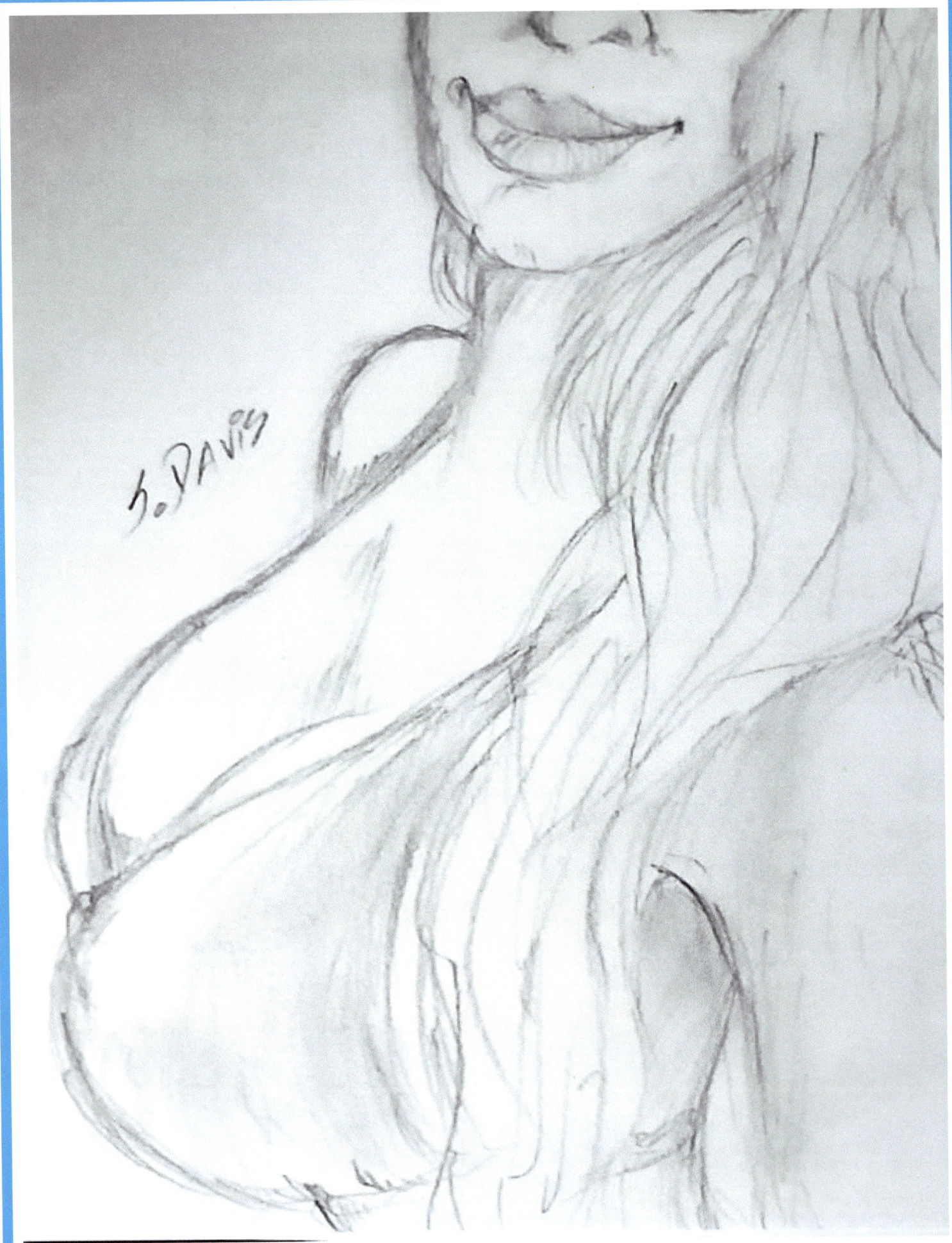

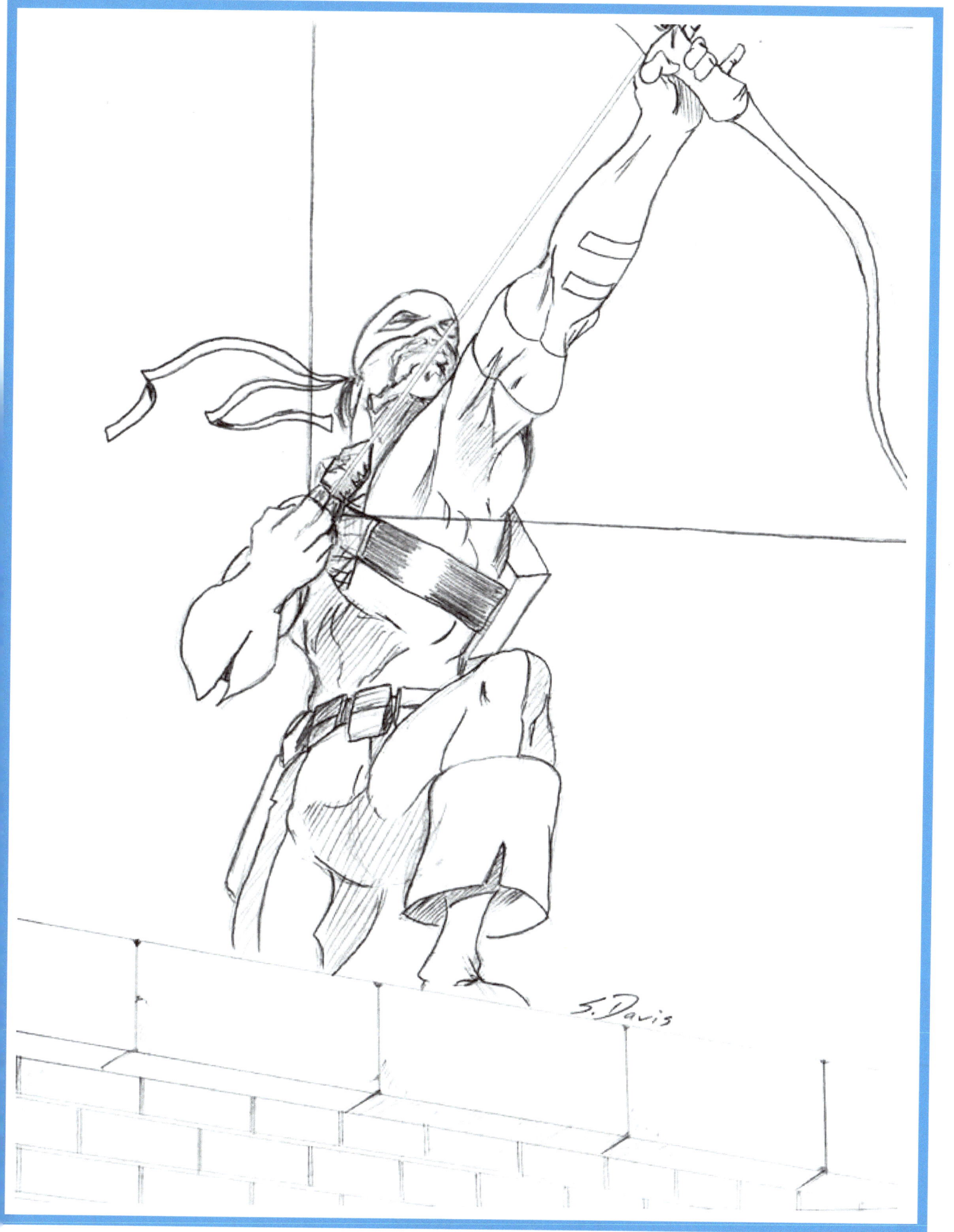

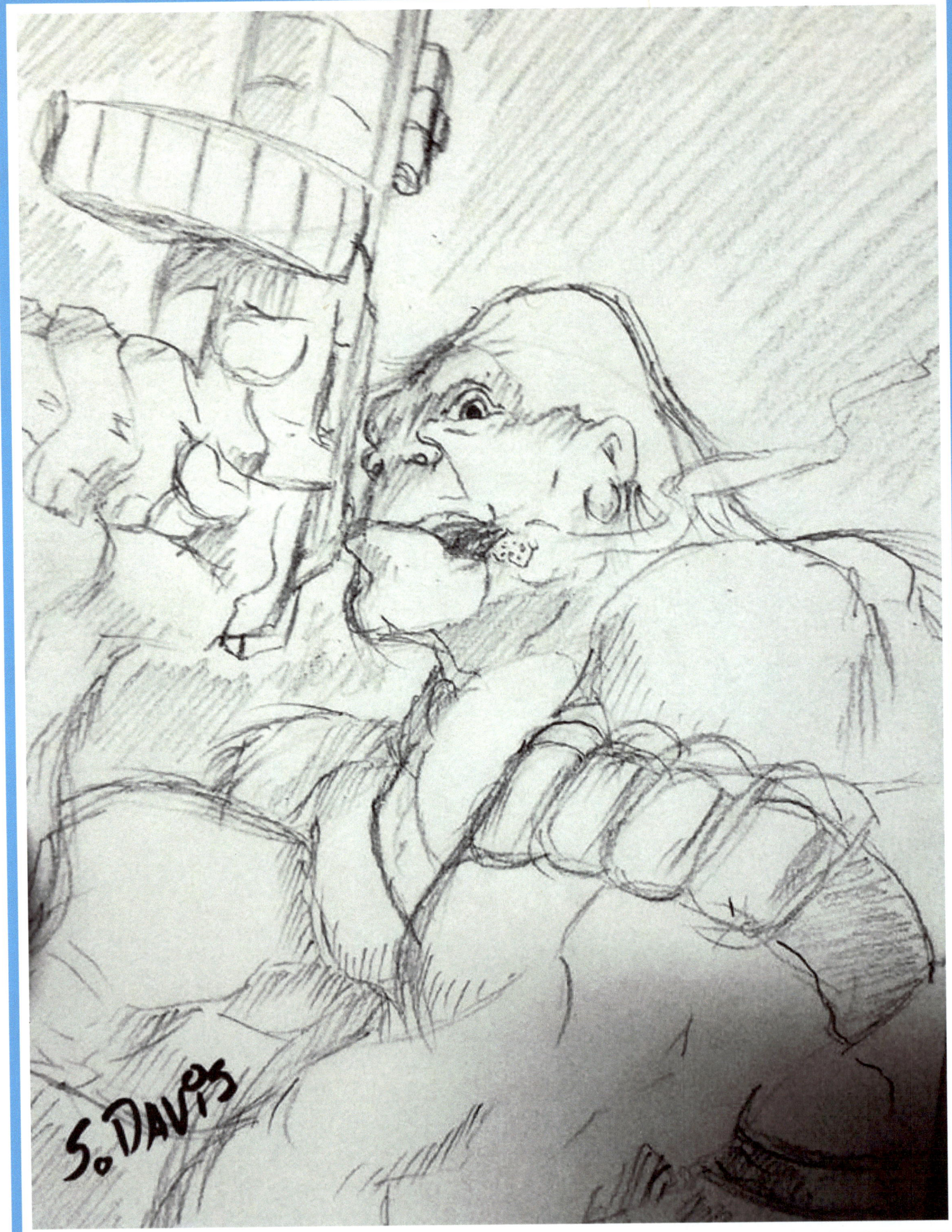

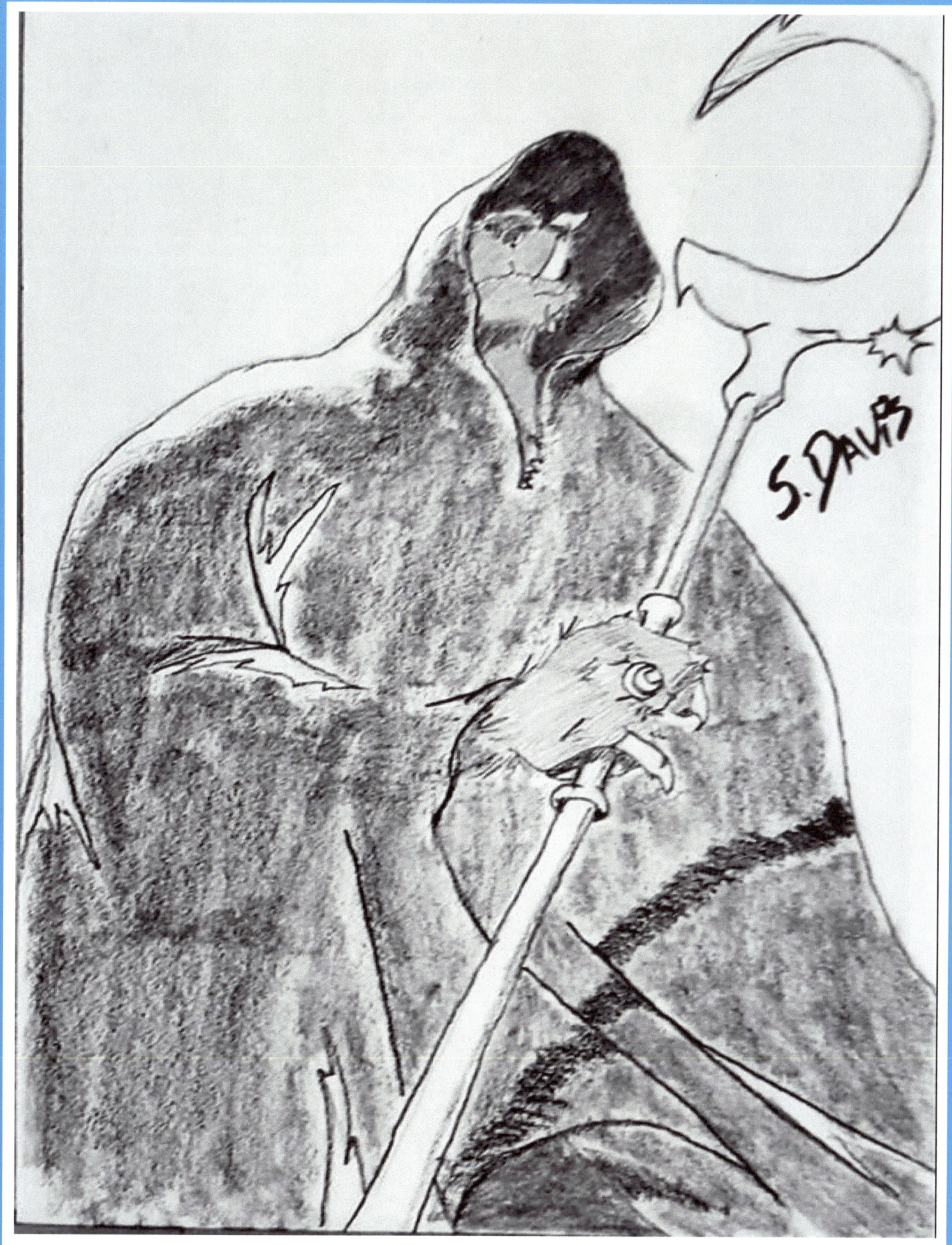

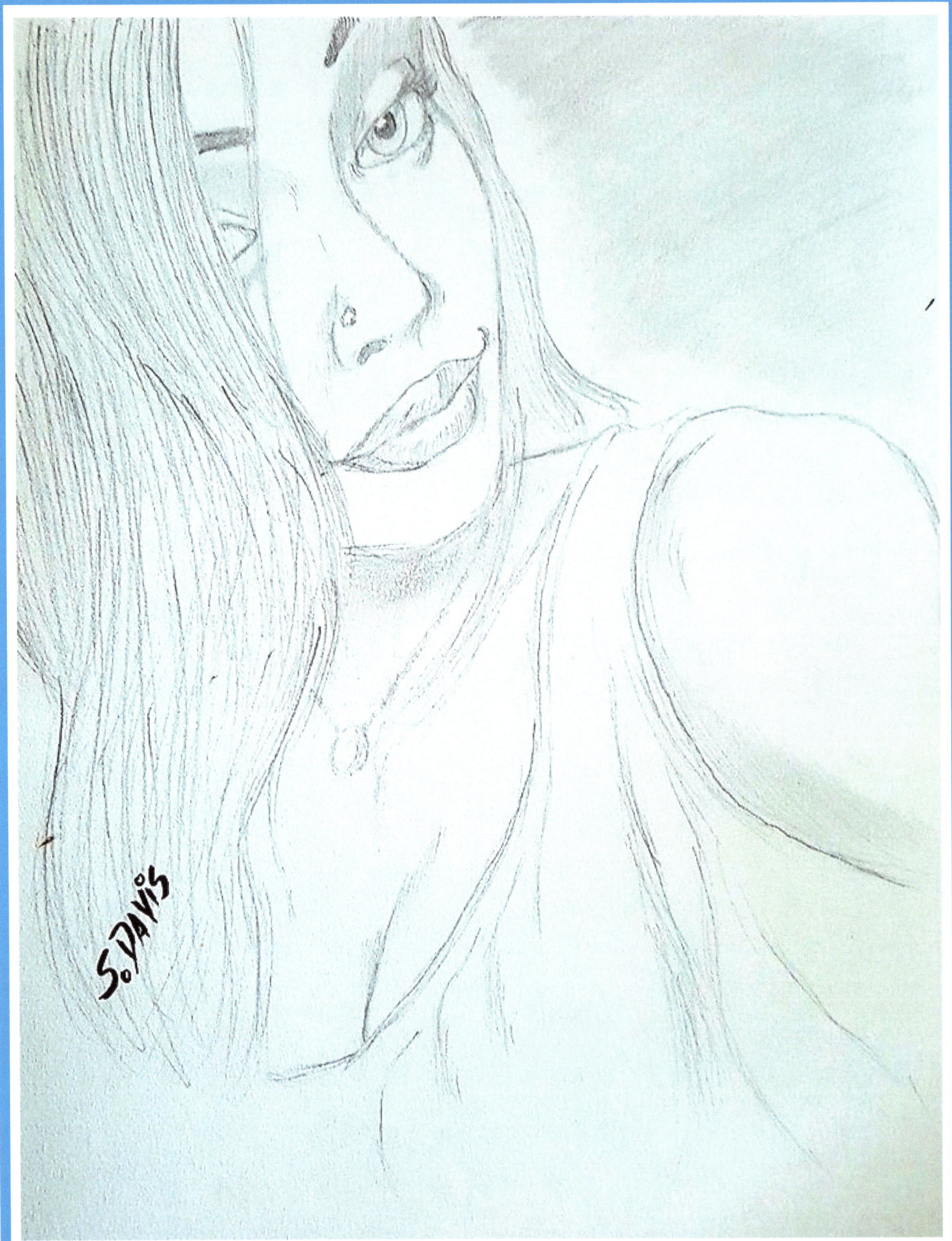

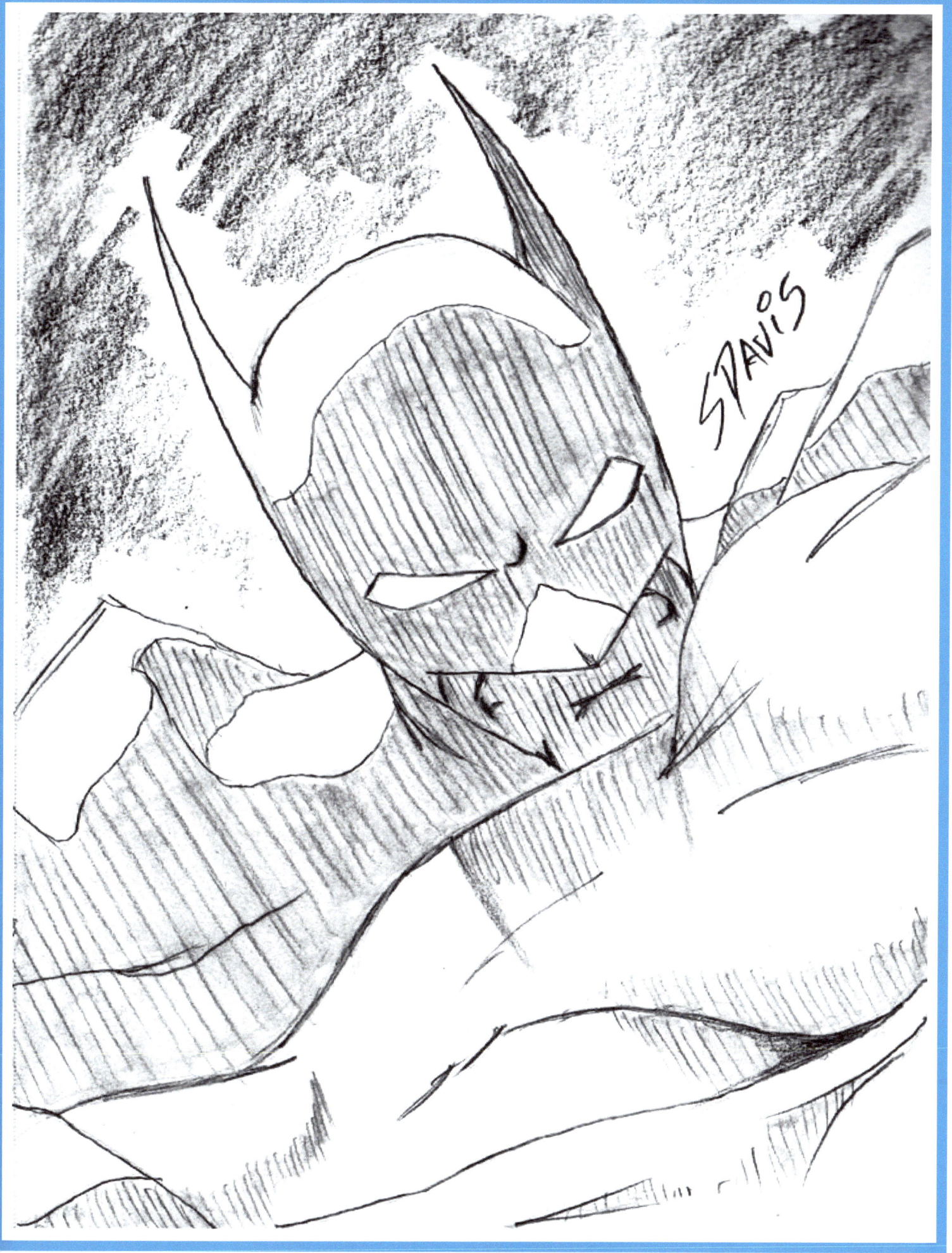

'BAT SPORK'

S.DAVIS

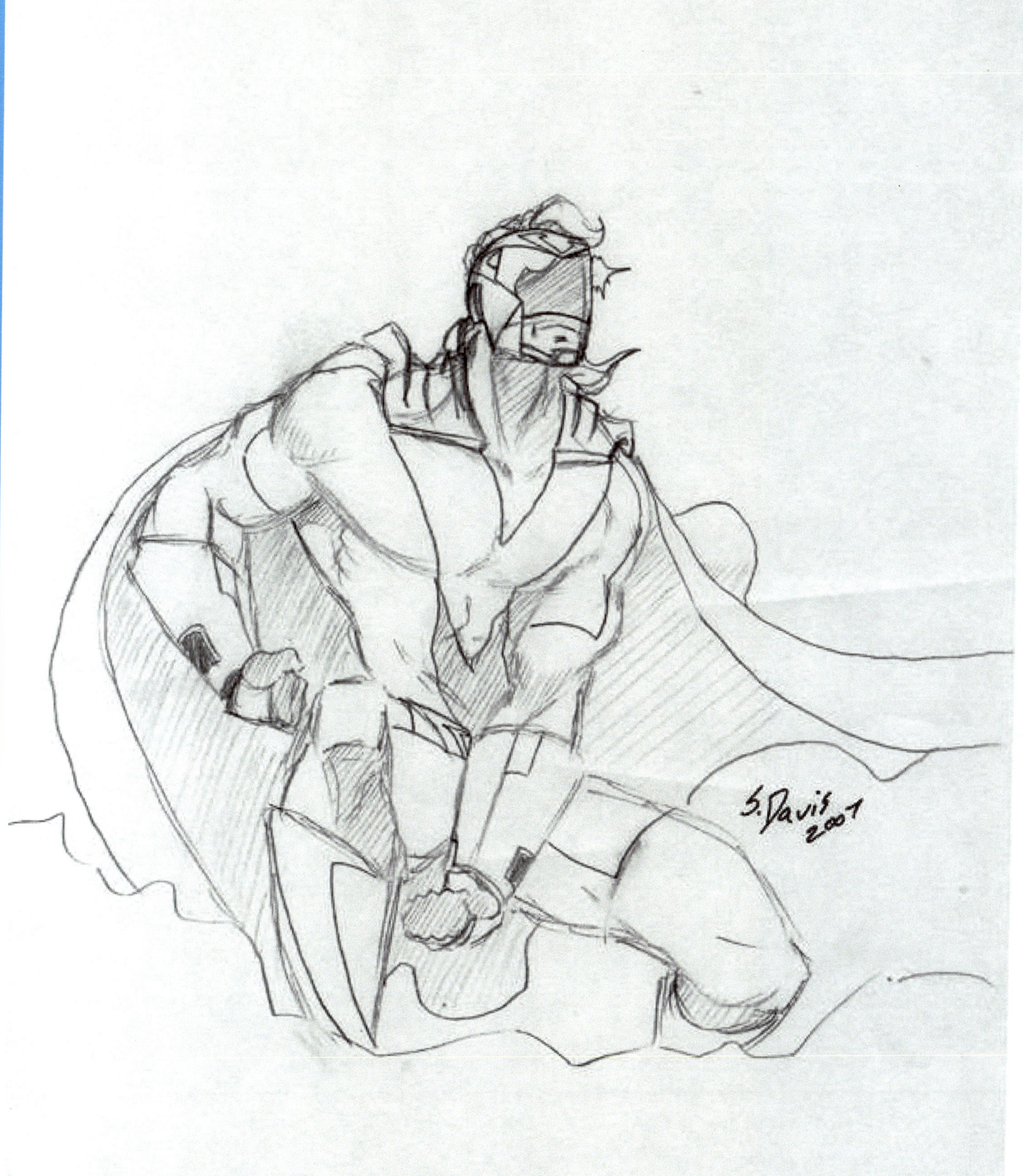

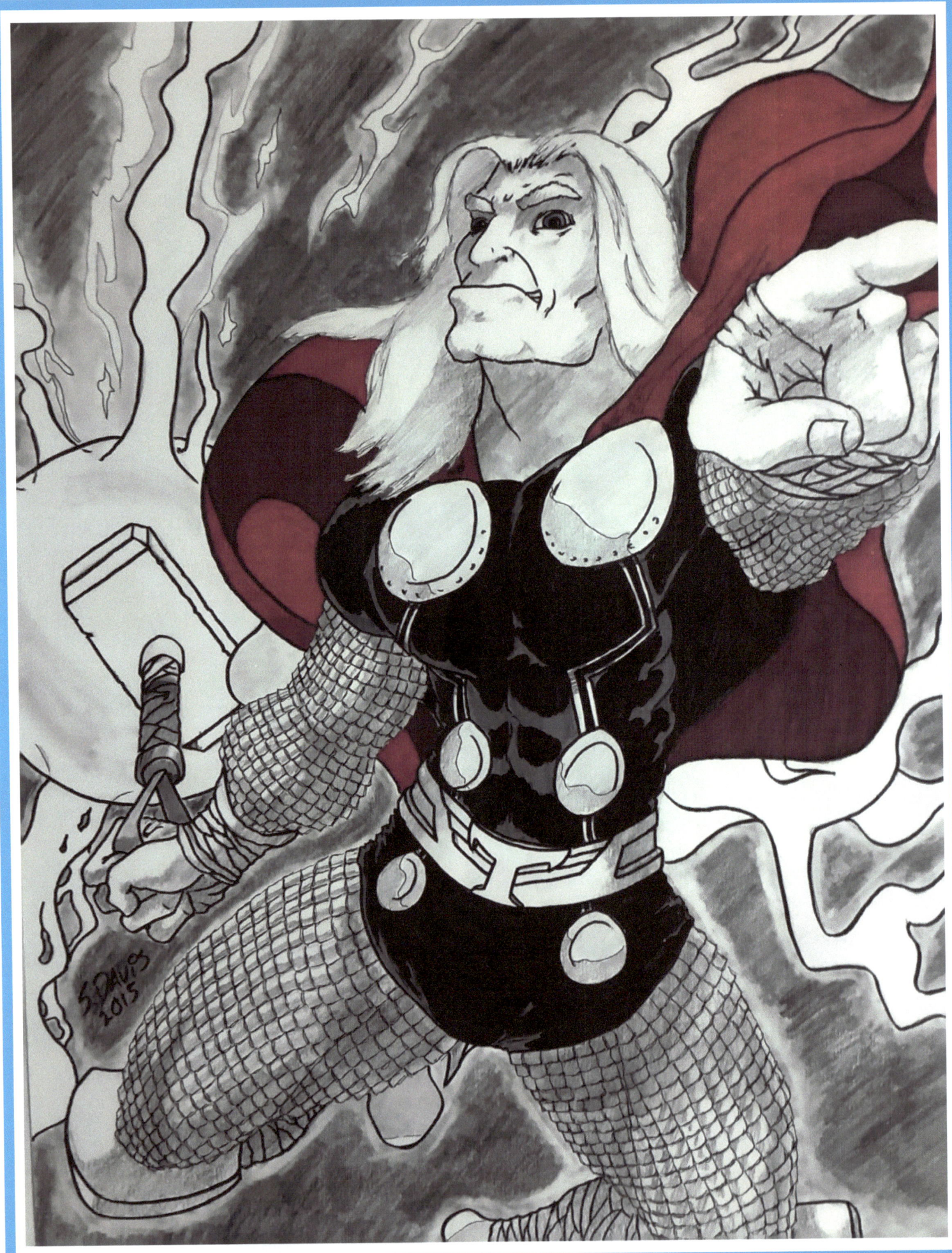

AS AN ADDED BONUS, THE NEXT FEW PAGES ARE AN EXERPT OF PANELS FROM A WORK IN PROGRESS TITLED:

# *VALIANT KNIGHTS

I CAN'T SAY MUCH ABOUT THE STORY AS IT IS A WORK IN PROGRESS, BUT I HOPE YOU ENJOY THEM AS I AM ENJOYING THE EVOLUTION OF THE CHARACTERS.

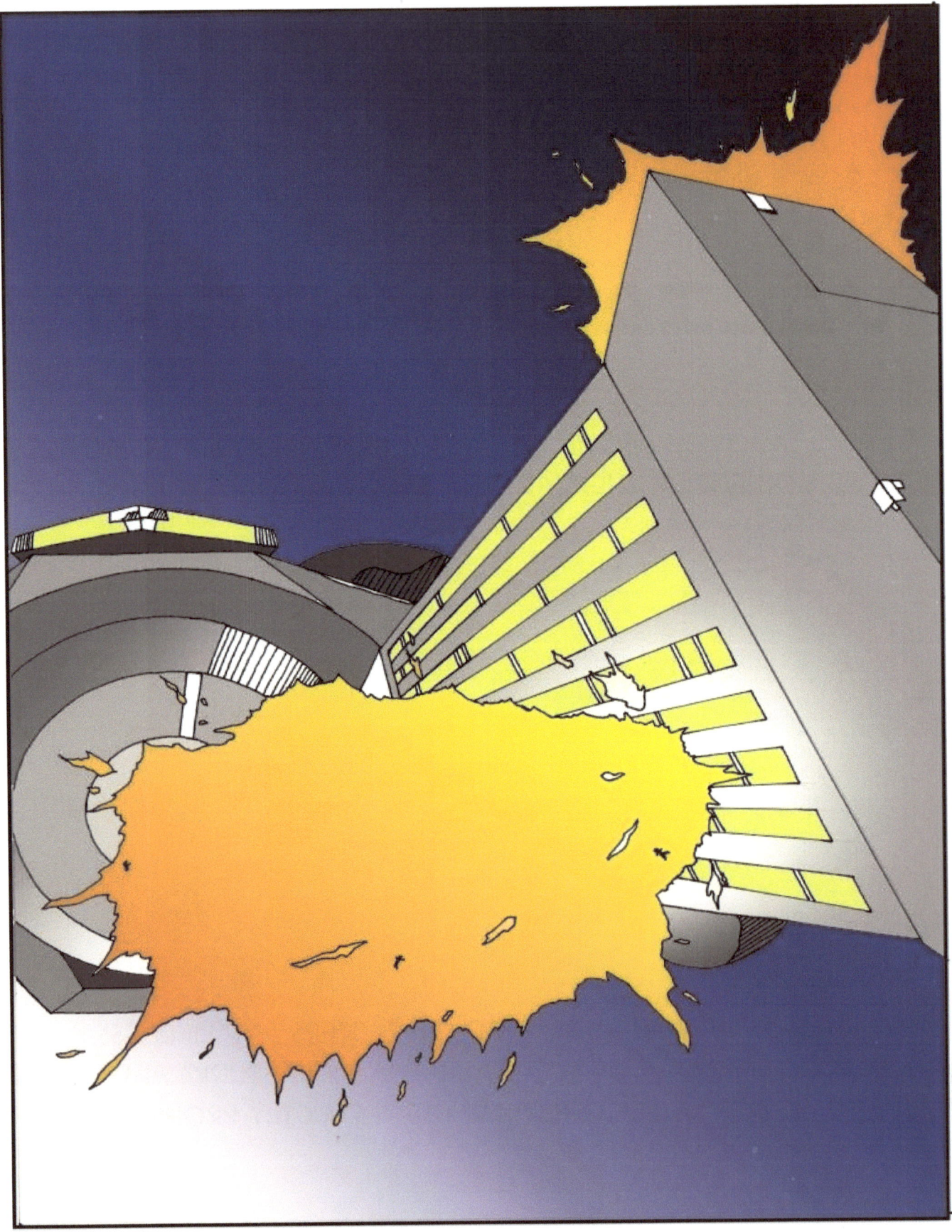

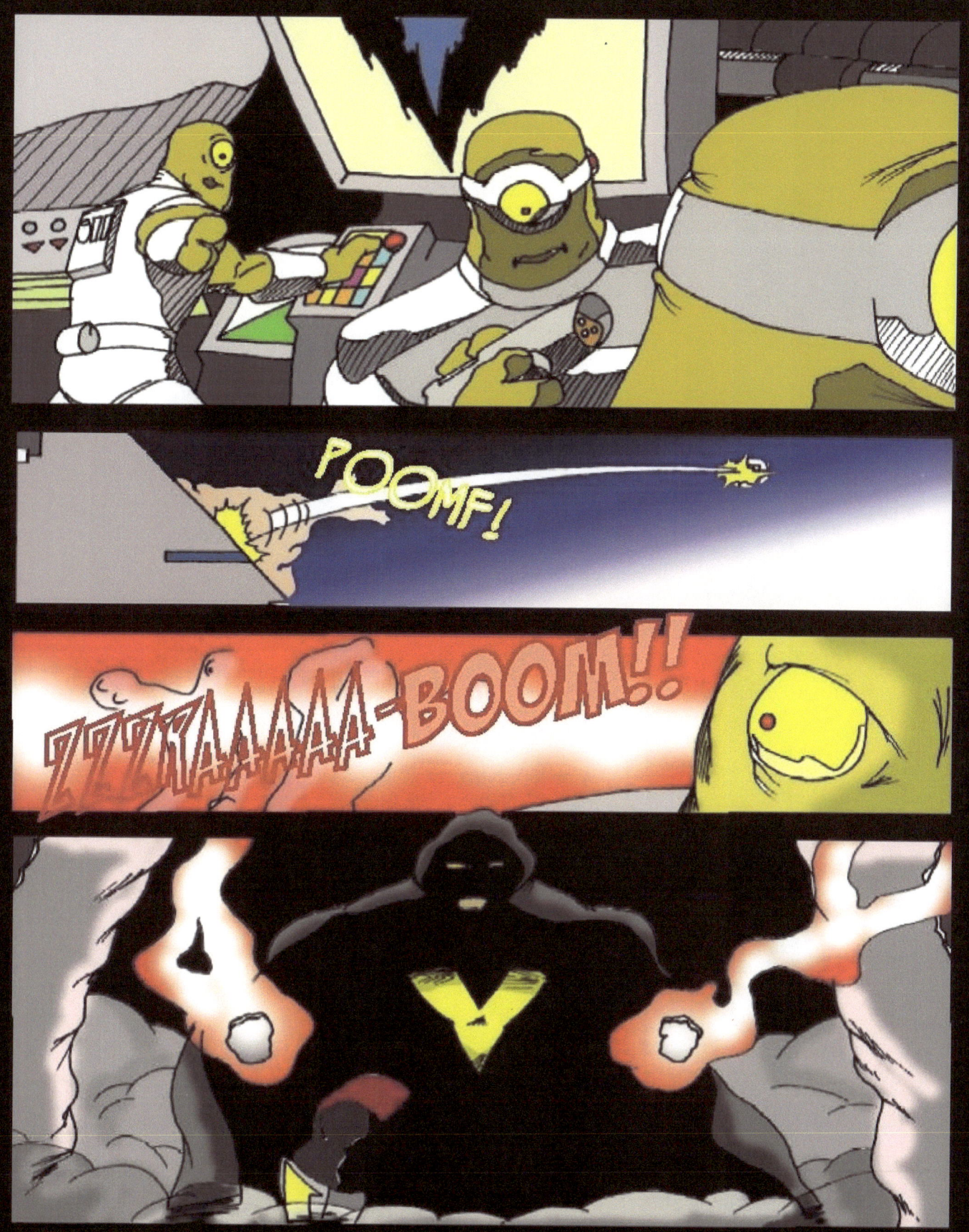

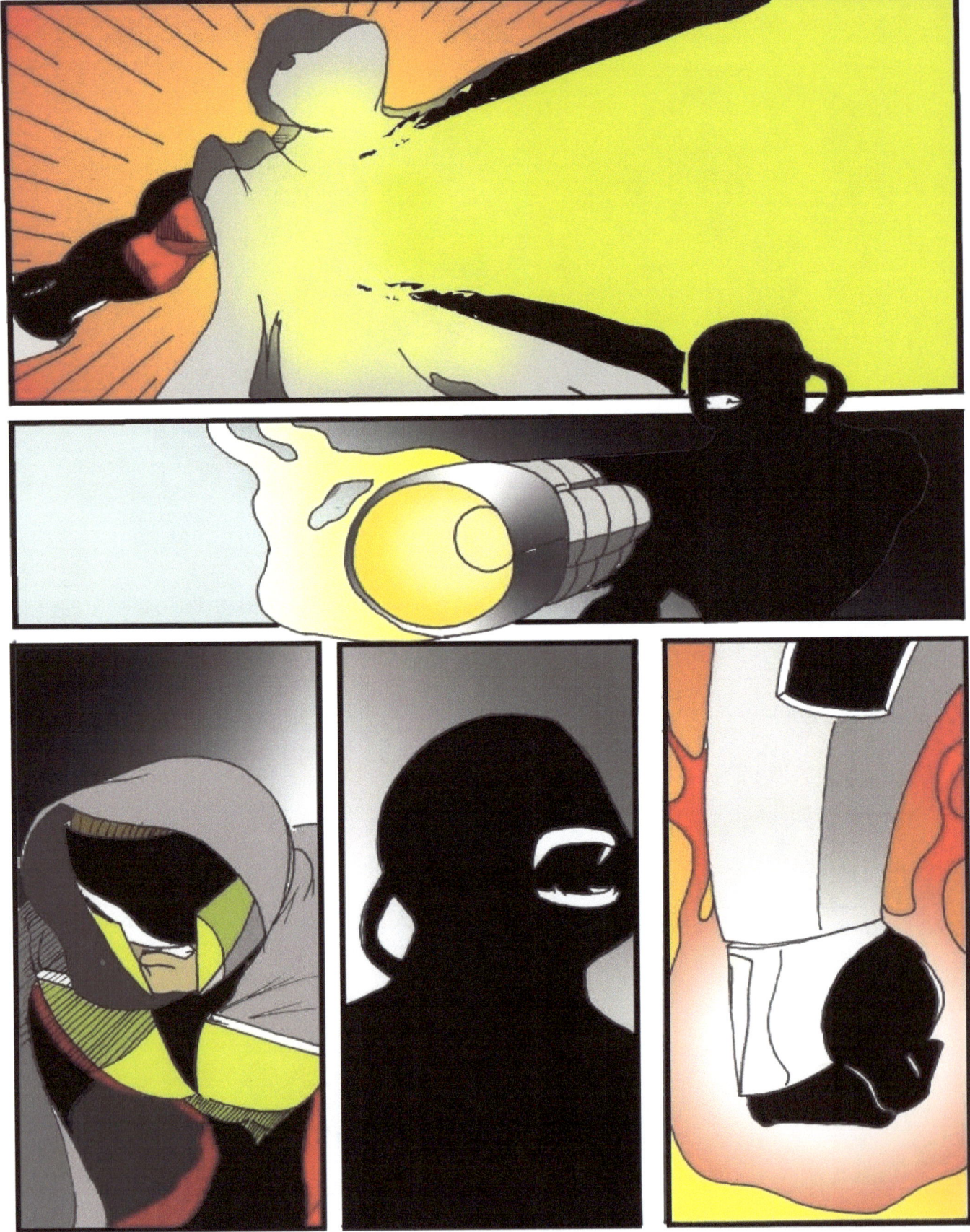

# THE END

## ...OR IS IT JUST THE BEGINNING!